Fact/Book
on
ARTHRITIS,
NUTRITION
and
NATURAL THERAPY

The Arthritis Patient's "Enemies" List
. . . and Some "Friends."

Enemies	*Friends*
Sugar	Cod liver oil
Wet feet	Pineapple
Aspirin	Hot wax
Meat	Sunlight
Bad posture	Vitamin E
	Organic foods
	Whirlpool baths

The "friends" and "enemies" listed above may not seem related to arthritis, but as this up-to-the-minute *Fact/Book* shows, there is abundant clinical evidence of the parts they play in the progress or prevention of our most implacable crippler.

Almost everyone who lives long enough will suffer the pains of arthritis — yet, for many, it is avoidable. This invaluable guide explores remedies and causes, preventive measures and palliatives, warning signs and practical advice, to give present and potential arthritis patients — and they may include you — and their friends and families the information they need to stave off or deal with this all-pervading disease.

Your own body has the will and the equipment to fight arthritis. This book will show how you can help it do just that.

Carlson Wade's

FACT/BOOK
ON
ARTHRITIS, NUTRITION and NATURAL THERAPY

Keats Publishing, Inc.

New Canaan, Connecticut

FACT/BOOK ON ARTHRITIS, NUTRITION AND NATURAL THERAPY

Pivot Original Health Edition published 1976
Copyright (c) 1976 by Carlson Wade

Printed in the United States of America

Library of Congress Catalog Card Number 76-24502

PIVOT ORIGINAL HEALTH BOOKS are published by
Keats Publishing, Inc.
36 Grove Street, New Canaan, Connecticut 06840

*For all those engaged in the battle
against arthritis,
this book was written
as a helpful weapon*

TABLE OF CONTENTS

INTRODUCTION

THE PURPOSE of this book is to help you cope with arthritis by using natural health programs including nutrition, sunshine, water, exercise and other home remedies. The number of arthritic sufferers is increasing steadily and it is important for everyone to become familiar with the many forms of the disease and with the variety of healing methods available for relief.

You must realize that improvement through natural home programs comes about slowly, and may take days, weeks or even months. Only resolve, determination, and faithful adherence to a program will bring results.

If you are troubled with arthritic pains, keep in mind these four goals when you follow the programs outlined in this book:

1) A reduction in pain and inflammation.
2) Increased mobility in arthritic joints.
3) Greater stability and dependability in joint function.
4) Functional improvement which will lead to increased self-sufficiency.

This book will guide you toward these goals. It is important to be aware that arthritis is one of the fastest-growing ailments of our time. As research clears away its mystery, various forms of healing are discovered. Slowly, the causes are identified and the hope for cure grows. This book presents some natural healing programs as they are used by specialists.

Here are some facts and figures about arthritis:

Arthritis is a term used to describe nearly 100 rheumatic diseases.

At least 50,000,000 Americans have some form of arthritic condition.

There are 20,230,000 victims of crippling arthritis in the United States.

- 600,000 new victims are claimed each year.
- 5,000,000 suffer from rheumatoid arthritis — the most crippling form of the disease.
- Rheumatoid arthritis usually strikes people in the 20 to 50 "prime-of-life" years.
- It strikes women 3 times as often as men.
- 12,000,000 people have osteoarthritis seriously enough to cause painful problems.
- 250,000 children are affected.
- Arthritis hits 1 of every 4 families, or 1 in 10 people.
- Almost $4 1/2 billion in wages and homemaker services are lost annually because of arthritis.
- Arthritics spend a half-billion dollars a year on medications that promise to give relief, often to no avail.

Because of this serious problem, researchers and scientists are investigating any possible cause, no matter how slight, in the hopes of unlocking the mystery of this crippling disease.

The following chapters report on the various discoveries concerning nutrition and home therapy that can give hope for real improvement.

CHAPTER 1.

THE MANY FACES OF ARTHRITIS

ARTHRITIS is often called "everybody's sneaky ailment" because it affects almost all of us in some way, physically or financially. Yet, most people have only vague ideas and incorrect information about the disease. As a result, they become crippled needlessly and remain crippled needlessly. They are misinformed about arthritis, its causes and its response to natural therapies, and remain ignorant of the medical discoveries regarding arthritis and nutrition. The simple fact is that most arthritics do not know the truth about their ailment. Nor are they aware of the value of corrective nutrition and home therapy linked with medical care as a means of accomplishing more than just easing pain — programs that can help to heal arthritis.

Let us take a closer look at arthritis. It means "inflammation of a joint." The name comes from the words *arth* (joint) and *itis* (inflammation). It is a condition that may appear from time to time in one's life as mild or occasional discomfort. Or it may press on relentlessly toward serious crippling and invalidism. The course arthritis takes depends on the nature of the arthritic condition (which may be mild or severe) and the person's own physical state. The word *arthritis* is also used to describe about one hundred different conditions which cause aching and pain in joints and connective tissues throughout the body; not all of these necessarily involve inflammation.

One point, however, needs to be heavily underscored: *The entire body is affected by arthritis, even though only the joints are involved.* Therefore, in treatment, the whole body must be considered.

THE HIGH COST OF ARTHRITIS

The total impact of arthritis on our population is startling. Whether mild or serious, it strikes people of all ages, from infancy onward. Almost everyone, if he lives long enough, will develop some form of the disease. The National Institute of Health reports that *97 percent of all persons over age 60 have arthritis that is visible in X rays.*

Arthritis is both crippling and costly as we see from these figures based on surveys conducted by the National Institute of Health of the U.S. Department of Health:

Annually:
- 3,500,000 arthritics disabled at a given time
- 240,000,000 days of restricted activity
- 15,000,000 days lost from work (regular job)
- 700,000 arthritics unable to work, keep house, attend school or participate in most recreational activities

Each year, enormous financial costs add to the burden of physical strain:
- $ 854,000,000 for hospitalization
- 493,000,000 for physicians' office visits
- 600,000,000 for prescription drugs
- 500,000,000 for non-prescription drugs
- 50,000,000 for services other than physician
- 26,000,000 for federal and private programs for arthritis

The grand total of yearly financial costs adds up to $2,931,000,000 — or almost $3 billion!

Indirect costs affecting the economy each year include:

- $3,512,000,000 for lost wages
- 974,000,000 for lost homemaker services
- 773,000,000 for lost federal, state and local income taxes because of lost earnings
- 316,000,000 for lost disability insurance payments
- 132,000,000 for aid to the permanently and totally disabled
- 194,000,000 for earnings lost because of premature death
- 394,000,000 for Veterans' Administration compensation

The grand total of yearly economic costs comes to $6,295,000,000 — or over $6 billion! The total cost of arthritis amounts to over $9 billion each year and the figures continue to soar. Arthritis has been called America's foremost crippling disease. The cost in human suffering, in pain and disability, is beyond measurement.

THE FORMS ARTHRITIS TAKES

Basically, *arthritis* refers to inflammation and destruction of joints, specifically, of their lining. *Rheumatism*, a more general term, usually refers to symptoms in tissues outside the joints, such as muscles, tendons, bones and nerves. These days, the names are synonymous. Let us now unmask this insidious thief of health and recognize its disguises.

Rheumatoid Arthritis. It is three times more prevalent in women than men. It usually begins between the ages of thirty-five and fifty, but people of all ages are susceptible, from early infancy through advanced age. Studies of its incidence in certain populations indicate that rheumatoid arthritis afflicts three out of every hundred people. Of these, one out of every three is very severely affected.

Rheumatoid arthritis is the most crippling of the

various types of arthritis. Although it does most of its damage to the joints, it primarily affects the body's connective tissues. (These tissues connect and support the specialized components and organs of the body and include membranes, tendons, ligaments, bone and cartilage.) Unchecked, rheumatoid arthritis can cause disease in the lungs, skin, blood vessels, muscles, spleen, heart and even the eyes.

Symptoms begin with general fatigue, soreness, stiffness and aching followed by the gradual appearance of localized symptoms (pain, swelling, warmth and tenderness) in a joint or in several joints. Sometimes, there is a *sudden* onset of these symptoms. In most cases, rheumatoid arthritis strikes several joints, especially those of the hands and feet.

The disease is characterized by inflammatory changes and swelling in the membrane lining the joint. Inflamed tissue forms over the joint surfaces, causing pain.

Symptoms also include loss of appetite, loss of weight and cold, sweaty hands and feet. They may come and go, with flare-ups alternating with periods of improvement. If allowed to progress untreated, rheumatoid arthritis may cause loss of joint motion and deformity.

It is in rheumatoid arthritis that emotions may have a profound effect upon the body's response to the arthritic threat. Worry, unhappiness or other emotional upset seems to bring on new attacks or make existing bouts worse. Attacks are usually symmetrical, that is, the same joints on both sides of the body are affected at about the same time. Unchecked, each recurring attack seems more severe and incapacitating until, in the end, the joints become permanently enlarged with only a small area of motion left. This unhappy condition need not occur if treatment is begun early.

Osteoarthritis. As the body ages it shows signs of life's wear-and-tear in many ways. Changes in vision and hearing loss are examples. In the body skeleton the most likely places to show this aging process are those parts that do the heaviest work — the weight-bearing joints. This type of joint inflammation is called osteoarthritis.

Basically, it is characterized by degeneration of joint cartilage. The moist surfaces at the ends of the bones that form the joint tend to become rough; after long and hard usage the joint becomes painful. It is said that nearly everyone develops osteoarthritis to some degree, and in one or more joints in the later years.

This disease of the joints involves the breakdown of cartilage and other tissues which make a movable joint operate properly. The damage from osteoarthritis is confined to the joints and surrounding tissues. There is little or no inflammation, but pain and limitation of normal motion sometime occur. The cartilage becomes soft, wears unevenly and, in some areas, may disappear completely, exposing the underlying bones. The bone ends also may thicken. The rest of the body is seldom affected and, except in some cases involving the hip joints, the ailment causes no noticeably severe deformity or crippling.

Osteoarthritis occurs primarily among middle-aged and elderly persons. It is more prevalent in women than in men. (Women frequently have their first symptoms at menopause.)

Since osteoarthritis seldom causes inflammation and does not affect the entire body, victims are often not bothered by it, even if there are some visible signs. Eventually there is pain, but this may be only a mild ache or soreness, especially with movement. Some people have constant nagging pain which persists even at rest. It is a slow progression. At first, soreness and stiffness are apparent only after the joint has had extra hard usage. Rest relieves the discomfort and soon the soreness is forgotten.

But with the passing of years and neglect, the soreness persists because the surfaces of the joint are injured. There is increasing stiffness. It is painful to use hands and those joints that bear the body's weight. The fingers often become enlarged around the last joint.

It is believed that chronic irritation of the joints is the main contributing factor to osteoarthritis. This may be the result of overweight, poor posture, injury or mechanical strain from one's occupation or routine activities. Osteoarthritis may also be caused by metabolic or endocrine (hormone-gland) abnormalities which weaken the joint cartilage, predisposing it to disease. Overweight people who stand or walk a great deal, overburdening their knees and hips, are especially susceptible.

Gout. Considered a metabolic ailment, it is now known to be associated with an increased amount of uric acid (a common chemical substance) in the blood and also in the tissues of those afflicted. It usually accumulates in the small joints, particularly the big toe.

Gout is characterized by its periodic and sudden occurrence. Usually it is easy to identify because the pain is acute and the joint very reddened and extremely tender. Joints other than the big toe may be affected. Men are the chief sufferers and it seems to run in families, usually making its first appearance around middle age. It is an abnormality of body chemistry.

Uric acid is manufactured as part of the normal life process. It is produced from substances called *purines*, which are found in many foods, but especially in animal organs such as sweetbreads, brains, kidney and liver. Beer is another purine source.

Normally, uric acid is discharged from the body in wastes. But some circumstances cause an accumulation of high levels of uric acid in the bloodstream and this in turn causes gout. Uric acid is relatively insoluble in body fluids. A gout attack is the result of precipitation of sodium urate in joint tissues.

Gout usually strikes men after middle age and women after the menopause. If gout is not treated, there may be degenerating function of the affected joints, especially the feet or hands. Permanent handicap can result.

It is important for gout patients to drink a lot of liquids such as water, fruit and vegetable juices. This cuts down the risk of developing kidney stones and also increases the discharge of uric acid. Three to five quarts of liquid a day are most helpful in enabling the body to rid itself of excess uric acid.

Ankylosing Spondylitis. Also called Marie-Strumpell Disease, this is an ailment of the spine, similar in many ways to rheumatoid arthritis. This type of arthritis, however, attacks men ten times more than women and nearly always begins in young adulthood.

First to be afflicted are the small joints of the spine and the sacroiliac (lower part of the back) with pain in the lower back and legs. Other joints, such as the shoulders and hips, may also be affected. Complications often cause eye inflammation. Spinal stiffness may increase, until the spine is completely rigid. In advanced cases, spinal curvature develops and the person is forced to walk in a stooped position. While progression may stop of its own accord after a few years, the stiffness remains and causes difficulty.

Psoriatic Arthritis. Psoriasis is a skin disorder in which reddish-brown areas or patches appear on the skin; these are soon covered with silvery white or grayish scales of dead skin which drop off. Affected areas may be only small circles on the scalp, elbows or knees or may cover the entire back or thighs. This condition affects more than 4,000,000 Americans. It is said that one out of every ten cases of psoriasis is complicated by a form of rheumatoid arthritis. Help for psoriatic arthritis is similar to that offered for rheumatoid arthritis.

Systemic Lupus Erythematosus (SLE). A collagen (cement substance that binds cells and tissues together) ailment that inflames and damages connective tissue throughout the body, SLE affects the skin, joints and internal organs. Its symptoms include skin rash, weight loss, fever, weakness, fatigue, joint pain, anemia and kidney problems. SLE strikes mostly young women (about five to one over men) of twenty to forty years of age but can occur at any age. SLE follows the same course as rheumatoid arthritis with its unpredictable periods of advancement and remission.

Discoid SLE. This is a degeneration of connective-tissue elements of the skin. *Disseminated SLE* may affect connective tissue anywhere throughout the body; the kidneys and other organs can be involved. In any form it takes, it is not to be disregarded but treated promptly.

Bursitis. This condition is defined as an inflammation of a bursa, the small fluid-filled sac which lies between a muscle and a bone or between two muscles. A cushioning device located at potential friction points between adjoining tissues within a joint structure, a bursa acts as a bearing to assist smooth, comfortable movement.

Irritation from injury or pressure can trigger inflammation of a bursa, causing extreme pain and tenderness. The entire joint may become red and swollen. Frequently, bursitis affects a shoulder but it can occur in other joints such as the elbows or hips. Prolonged use of a joint which a bursa serves (such as the elbow in tennis) may cause bursitis, since the bursa is a pocket of fibrous tissue lined in the same way as a joint with a slippery synovial (lubricating fluid) membrane; prolonged and unusual use of the joint can inflame the bursa.

Rheumatic Fever. A generalized inflammatory ailment affecting the entire body and symptomized by pain and swelling of the joints, rheumatic fever is often caused by a streptococcus (microbe or bacteria) infection and it is damaging to the heart. It is considered an arthritic ailment because it inflames joints. Though painful, it is not crippling and should clear up with proper treatment. Inflammation and scarring of the heart valve is a common result and is called rheumatic heart disease. The fever usually follows a sore throat or tonsillitis caused by the streptococcus germ, but it is not a "strep" infection. The damage to heart valves from rheumatic fever is permanent. Because rheumatic fever tends to recur, it should be treated promptly.

Fibrositis. Not a specific ailment, but a name given to a combination of unexplained aches and pains and stiffness in various parts of the body, fibrositis is familiarly known as muscular rheumatism. It is unrelated to joints or body movements. Instead, it strikes weak, nervous or tense people and it is more acute in those who are emotionally upset, tired or excited. Fibrositis pain comes and goes for no apparent reason. Faulty posture (which could affect either the backbone or the muscles where the pain is felt) is an important factor in bringing on an attack as is an awkward sitting position or sitting stiffly in any position. Tension, which includes anxiety, may also predispose its occurrence. Often, the pain may be eased by relaxing the body and avoiding awkward and unhealthy sitting, walking, standing or sleeping postures.

Fibrositis is an inflammation of the white fibrous connective tissue that forms muscle sheaths and merges into muscle attachments. It also is the term used for any soft-tissue disorder that causes aches and pains in and around the muscles and joints. Tendon sheaths and bursae may also be involved. Often, the muscle that runs over the top of the shoulder is affected, becoming stiff and painful.

Scleroderma. This is an ailment of the body's connective tissues with accompanying symptoms of arthritis. The skin hardens and thickens and there may be accompanying inflammation and scarring of muscles and internal organs. It strikes more women than men; while it can begin at any age, it is more frequent in the forties and fifties. It may progress rapidly or vary in severity for years.

Infectious Arthritis. Arthritis often follows an infection. Bacteria can penetrate the joints and cause acute or chronic forms of arthritis. Tuberculosis and pneumonia, for instance, may precipitate arthritis in both youngsters and adults. Syphilis also produces arthritis. A particularly painful form is gonorrheal arthritis, which was once common and very crippling.

It used to be thought that the continued presence of abscessed teeth and tonsils and similar "focal" or local infections caused arthritis but this is questionable. Medical care may suggest removal of these pockets of infection on the grounds of general health, but such removal will not have much influence on coexisting arthritis.

ARTHRITIS WARNING SIGNS
1. Persistent pain and stiffness upon arising
2. Pain or tenderness in one or more joints
3. Swelling in one or more joints
4. Recurrence of these symptoms, especially when they involve several joints
5. Pain and stiffness in the neck, lower back, knees and other joints
6. Tingling sensations in the fingertips, hands and feet

7. Unexplained weight loss, fever, weakness or fatigue

Alert Yourself to Arthritis. This ailment is not a dramatic killer like heart disease. But it has the slow and certain malignancy of cancer. It is a "chronic" condition. It afflicts more people than any other chronic disease. Its one common symptom is steadily worsening pain. (Often, early arthritis brings very mild, unnoticed pain.) Symptoms may come and go with no apparent cause.

Arthritis can cause grave illness, create excruciating pain and lead to deformities of the hands, fingers, wrists, knees, feet, toes and hips. It can make bedridden invalids. It can shatter families and drain financial savings. Arthritis is a serious ailment. Alert yourself to its signs and use whatever nature provides to correct its cause and thereby ease and combat its symptoms.

CHAPTER 2.

ASPIRIN, DRUGS AND CHEMICAL TREATMENTS

"TROUBLED WITH ARTHRITIS? Reach for an aspirin!"

This invitation to freedom from arthritic pain is extended to everyone through radio, television, newspaper and magazine advertising and even billboards. In truth, aspirin (along with other drugs) can make the problem much worse. These patent medicines mask symptoms and give an illusion of healing. Actually, arthritis progresses while the pain (nature's warning signal) is drugged. Medication has to be increased as pain increases. Only when the aspirin-taker becomes crippled, is it realized that drugs have created a delusion of healing, easing the pain but not halting the progression of the ailment.

Each day, 36 million aspirins are swallowed! By the time you finish this chapter, *more than half a million aspirins will be taken*, for better or (most likely) for worse.

Aspirin is a drug. Even though it is easily available without prescription, over the counter, it is not without its risks and side effects.

About 400,000 people have reactions to aspirin, yet may be unaware of their allergy. So says Kenneth F. Lampe, M.D., Professor of Pharmacology at the University of Miami School of Medicine, in the *Journal of the AMA* (23 Sept. 1974). Just one single dose of aspirin, says Dr. Lampe, can cause a reaction ranging from a slight cough with difficulty in breathing to a severe asthmatic attack. Skin eruptions, facial-tongue swelling, palm itching-burning sensations, and irritations on the scalp and soles of the feet may also result.

Dr. Lampe singles out people in the thirties and forties who are intolerant of aspirin and may contract cold-like symptoms with no pain or discomfort. Even after the runny nose has stopped, bronchial asthma may develop as a result of aspirin-taking.

"In almost every *fatal* outcome," says Dr. Lampe, "the patient was aware of his sensitivity but was told by his physician that one or two tablets never hurt anyone!"

Two typical pain-fever relieving ingredients in aspirins are *indomethacin* and *aminopyrine*, also known for causing reactions ranging from sniffles to serious respiratory ailments.

Internal bleeding and ulcers are extreme but frequent results of taking aspirin. It is estimated that more than 20,000 quarts of blood are lost by all the stomachs subjected to aspirin in just one day. While this may add up to only a few drops of blood per person, it is serious. Any form of internal bleeding is serious. Aspirin in amounts ranging from three to nine tablets daily may cause gastrointestinal bleeding in seven out of ten people, according to Harvey J. Weiss, M.D., in the *JAMA* (26 Aug. 1974).

Aspirin can cause gastric ulcers, reports Morton I. Grossman, M.D., a specialist in stomach and intestinal ailments from UCLA. At the 1974 World Congress of Gastroenterology, Dr. Grossman stated that one out of every three people suffering from gastric ulcers is a chronic user of aspirin.

An alert is issued by Micha Levy, M.D., in the *New England Journal of Medicine* (23 May 1974) to the effect that "causal relations exist between regular heavy aspirin intake and both major upper gastrointestinal bleeding and benign gastric ulcer."

Aspirin leaves the stomach wall vulnerable to ulceration by weakening the mucous barrier, says Hugh H. Hussey, M.D., in the *JAMA* (29 Apr. 1974). Not only is the stomach rendered susceptible to ulceration but *any* organ of the body that comes in contact with the aspirin before it is fully digested is subject to possible ulceration.

Furthermore, ingredients in aspirin inhibit blood clotting by reducing the adhesive power of blood platelets. This means that if the blood platelets cannot join to form a clot, bleeding continues. This can be more serious for people with anemia or iron deficiency.

Speaking before the International Symposium on Phenacetin Abuse in Vienna in 1974, Dr. Ranjit S. Nanra of the Royal New Castle Hospital in Australia explained that when aspirin is taken in large amounts over a long period of time, it can cause "irreparable damage to kidney tissue." Rheumatoid arthritis patients were found to have kidney damage in six out of every ten examined cases. All had a history of aspirin consumption. In some severe cases, kidney failure had occurred because of aspirin abuse.

Your liver can also be injured through taking aspirin carelessly. So reports H. J. Zimmerman, M.D., of the VA Hospital in Washington, D.C., in *Annals of Internal Medicine* (January 1974) from studies made over many years. In one typical case described in this journal, a twenty-year-old woman with diagnosed systemic lupus erythematosus (inflammation disease of the connective tissues) was put on high-dose aspirin therapy and subsequently developed hepatitis. When aspirin was removed, the hepatitis cleared up. But when she went back to aspirin, her liver reacted and the hepatitis returned.

In other reported cases, patients who developed liver dysfunction were taken off aspirin and improved their condition. All of these patients were troubled with arthritis which they hoped could be relieved by aspirin.

Dr. Zimmerman says that aspirin-induced liver dysfunction and injury could be cleared up after the drug was removed. "Nevertheless, a drug that produces hepatocellular injury (liver trouble) . . . must be suspected of being able to produce even more severe parenchymal injury (injury to part of an organ) on occasions."

A combination of aspirin with other drugs can cause a risky interaction. For example, if you take anticoagulants (to protect against blood clots), the mixture with aspirin could reduce your blood's ability to coagulate. A combination of antidiabetic drugs with aspirin can cause a serious drop in blood sugar levels. Aspirin with corticosteroids (hormone preparation used for allergies and other ailments) can predispose ulcer formation. Arthritic gout medicine (uricosurics) taken with aspirin can reduce its effectiveness. If aspirin and alcohol are combined, gastrointestinal bleeding can be increased.

Another hazard caused by the use of aspirin is its effect upon the heart, and the relationship between aspirin and the heart is under question by many specialists. It is believed that chemicals in aspirin may inhibit full heart health and are best avoided.

ADDITIONAL HEALTH RISKS

Aspirin as well as patent medicines containing aspirin are perilous for those who are troubled with gastric bleeding and stomach ulcers, according to medical specialists who testified at a Senate Monopoly Subcommittee hearing in June 1973 (*New York Times*, 6 June 1973).

"Aspirin is potentially capable of inducing severe gastric upset, acute ulceration of gastric and duodenal mucous membrane, aggravation of preexistent or latent gastric and duodenal peptic ulcer, initiation of fresh ulceration and precipitation of chronic or acute massive gastroduodenal hemorrhage," says Elliot L. Sagall, M.D., director of medical education for the American Trial Lawyers Association (*Trial*, March 1969).

Aspirin compounds can cause skin problems. It was found that in several women who had used an ointment containing 5 percent acetylsalicylic acid (an aspirin ingredient) to relieve the itching of psoriasis the skin condition worsened and they suffered hearing loss as well (*New England Journal of Medicine*, January 1966).

Aspirin alters the albumin (blood protein) factor of the bloodstream. In a talk before the 28th Annual Congress of the American College of Allergists in California in 1972, Richard S. Farr, M.D., said that according to tests, aspirin alteration of the albumin molecules is so severe, they remain in this form for as long as six weeks after a quantity of aspirin is taken.

"Aspirin may influence initiation of arteriothrombosis (heart trouble) . . . because platelet function tests were regularly abnormal in the aspirin group and unchanged in the placebo group," says J. R. O'Brien, M.D., of St. Mary's Hospital in Portsmouth, England. Aspirin inhibits the release of ADP (blood-clotting factor) and thereby destroys the blood platelets' ability to adhere to one another and interferes with good heart function as well as general body health (*Lancet*, 2 Sept. 1972).

Aspirin can also weaken and destroy the function of the little-known but highly important life-building substances known as *prostaglandins*. These are hormone-like ingredients that help lower high blood pressure, control ulcer-causing gastric juices, create better ventilation for respiration and even become involved in fertility. Aspirin turns off prostaglandin production; it inhibits the synthesis of certain prostaglandins which control the body's inflammatory response. While aspirin will create an antipyretic reaction (fever reduction) it also nullifies prostaglandin manufacture and the entire body may react adversely (*Nature*, December 1972, January 1973).

Aspirin is a drug and, as such, should be taken only with a doctor's guidance. To help ease any shock to the system caused by aspirin, liquids such as water or fruit and vegetable juices should be taken in quantity with the drug if, in an emergency, it must be used at all.

CREAMS THAT PROMISE TO
EASE ARTHRITIC PAIN

Externally applied creams purport to bring quick relief for arthritic pain. Are they effective? According to *Medicine Show*, published by Consumers Union, many of these sprays, ointments and rubs contain *methyl salicylate* (oil of wintergreen) as a major ingredient. Many use other ingredients which can be irritants. This source says:

"Application of these external analgesics tends to increase blood flow in the upper layers of the skin, resulting in a slight reddening of the skin as well as a sensation of warmth. This mild increase in skin temperature may provide symptomatic relief for a brief period.

"However, CU's medical consultants warn against the indiscriminate use of external analgesics with high methyl salicylate content. According to *The Pharmacological Basis of Therapeutics*, edited by Drs. Louis S. Goodman and Alfred Gilman, absorption of methyl salicylate can occur through the skin and can result in systemic toxicity.

"Absorption is speeded up if the drug is applied to mucous membrane or to areas where the skin is cut or inflamed. The use for children of preparations containing this drug should be strongly discouraged.

"A note of caution to the user of any external analgesic: A heating pad should never be used in conjunction with a liniment or external analgesic. Severe burns with blistering may result."

If you feel the need for an external ointment, ask your physician about the use of *pure* oil of wintergreen, alone, mixed with no other ingredient, a natural herbal preparation available at most herbal pharmacies. It should soothe the pain and make you feel more comfortable.

CORTISONE: CAUTION AHEAD

As a "miracle drug" cortisone is frequently used to lessen arthritic pain although it does not heal the cause, nor does it claim to do so. Cortisone is a synthetic drug patterned after the structure of a hormone formed in the cortex of the adrenal glands. It should be used with caution.

Peter Wingate, M.D., issues these words of warning in the *Penguin Medical Encyclopedia*: "Corticosteroids (cortisone preparations), affecting as they do many of the chemical processes of the body, have numerous undesirable effects if they are given over long periods.

"Healing, which depends on inflammation, is impaired, and wounds, gastric ulcers and the like become very troublesome. Bone and fibrous connective tissue are weakened, the patient puts on weight (much of it retained water), his blood pressure rises. As one would expect, the symptoms of prolonged treatment with large doses of corticosteroids are like those of overactivity of the adrenal glands (Cushing's syndrome)."

Dr. Wingate emphasizes that giving cortisone drugs over a long period "suppresses the natural activity of the adrenal cortex. If the treatment is suddenly stopped, the patient is left with no (natural) adrenal hormones and develops symptoms of Addison's disease (adrenal gland disorder)."

The Arthritis Foundation also says, "Cortisone and related steroid drugs are a special problem. They can bring about sensational reduction of pain and inflammation in a matter of hours. The disabled patient suddenly becomes able-bodied again. But steroids have been found to have serious side effects, sometimes worse than the rheumatoid disease. And steroids do not stop the disease process. They merely hide the fact that joint damage is still going on. So although they are still very useful in special situations, they are being prescribed less and less often by arthritis specialists today in the routine treatment of rheumatoid arthritis."

In situations that have been reported, the use of cortisone may cause a demineralization of the skeleton, an imbalance of the body's glandualar balance and a predisposition to possible onset of diabetes, ulcers and visual distress.

ARTHRITIS DRUGS THAT CONCEAL
BUT DO NOT HEAL

Several medications are used to help ease arthritic discomfort. While they do kill the pain, they conceal the disease without healing it. They may also cause serious side effects that will undermine the health of the arthritic which is usually below par to begin with. These arthritis remedies should be considered with caution.

Gold Salts. Specifically, they have been used to reduce the severity of rheumatoid inflammation. But they cause toxic reactions and the slightest overdose, however miniscule, can be dangerous. They do not work effectively for all arthritics.

Phenylbutazone. An analgesic drug that is said to offer temporary relief from inflammation, it does not have any effect on the slow, steady progression of arthritis. While it may offer relief from pain and stiffness, its side effects make it questionable for automatic acceptance.

Antimalarials. Because these drugs are derived from quinine, they are called antimalarials. While they do nothing to combat progressive arthritis they do reduce its symptoms. However, they must be prescribed for use over a very long period of time and can cause side effects such as anemia, blurred vision and skin and hair problems.

Indomethacin. An analgesic drug that is said to reduce pain and inflammation along with other symptoms, it is especially prescribed for spondylitis, osteoarthritis (of the hip, particularly) and gout. But it, too, has various side effects and long-term use may cause various ailments. It masks symptoms, but little else.

Both phenylbutazone and indomethacin can cause upset stomach, dizziness, blood thinning and skin and hair problems.

Patent medicines and drugs provide an illusion of relief; they have their purpose in providing symptom reduction but they do not purport to heal arthritis. As stated earlier, they may bring a feeling of improvement while the body deteriorates. By correcting the *cause* of arthritis, namely an error in metabolism, there is hope for erasing the problem without addiction to potentially harmful drugs.

CHAPTER 3.

CORRECTIVE NUTRITION

WHEN the body's metabolism goes awry, illness may result, often in the form of arthritis. Many physicians have found that when they supervise corrective nutrition, they can help change metabolism and improve arthritic conditions.

To begin with, it is important to review the way that arthritis works to better understand the importance of nutrition as a form of cure. Arthritis attacks a joint, slowly destroying its surrounding cartilage and dehydrating its lubricating oil. When this happens, bones are forced to rub against one another and this results in severe ache and inflammation. Unchecked or untreated, the joint gradually becomes stiff and often crippled. To correct this error or malfunctioning of metabolism, proper nutrition will give the body the materials needed to adjust the various systems.

Doctors report that nutritional therapy is not an overnight healer. It is a prolonged process requiring cooperation and patience from the arthritic. Since every case is different, the duration of a therapy diet varies. But it is reported that proper nutrition can halt the progress of the ailment and even reverse its course.

THE RAW FOOD DIET FOR ARTHRITIS
A diet of raw foods has been helpful in easing and

healing arthritic pain, according to Dorothy C. Hare, M.D. (British journal, *Proceedings of the Royal Society of Medicine*, Vol. 30). Dr. Hare does *not* advise a raw foot diet as a replacement for medication. But she reports that the following diet, which she supervised in Royal Free Hospital in England, helped many of her arthritic patients.

Breakfast: Apple porridge made of grated apple, soaked raw oatmeal, grated nuts, cream, fresh orange, tea with milk and cream.

Mid-morning: Tomato puree with lemon.

Dinner: Salad of lettuce, cabbage, tomato, root vegetables, oil-based salad dressing, mixed fruit salad, cream.

Teatime: Dried fruits, nuts, tea with milk and cream.

Supper: Fruit porridge, prune, apricot or apple salad with dressing.

Bedtime: Orange-lemon juice in boiled water.

Basic Program: For two weeks, the entire diet consisted of the preceding raw foods. Then, certain cooked foods (vegetable soup, one egg daily, two ounces of meat, two ounces of bread, butter, cheese and milk) were added to the basic raw foods. No salt was used for either raw or cooked foods. The dried fruits and raw oatmeal were soaked in water. All vegetables were shredded. Nuts were either whole or chopped. All food was prepared fresh for each meal. Servings were attractive.

Dr. Hare reports that within four weeks, eight out of the twelve patients showed much improvement. (Two were helped but then went into a relapse; two showed no change at all.) Of the eight patients, seven showed continued improvement after going home.

One forty-six-year-old arthritic with a four-year history of pain and swelling had been bedridden for ten weeks. She had fluid in both knee joints; there was painful swelling in other joints. The raw food diet gave her so much relief that she could do housework without any pain.

Dr. Hare says that nearly all were able to enjoy freedom from arthritic pain on this raw food diet. She attributes its success to "the absorption of the unaltered solar energy of plant life . . . . Science has so far revealed nothing . . . of this occult solar energy, as something apart from vitamin and chemical constituents of food." This suggests that nature-created substances in raw plant foods may be able to correct body metabolism and reduce arthritic distress.

The diet is high in vitamins A, B-complex and C. To make up for its low protein and fat content, Dr. Hare suggests the use of cream, nuts and salad oil; later, meat, eggs and cheese supply protein and other needed nutrients. Also the diet is low in sodium (but adequate in potassium) and this seems to be helpful to arthritics.

THE COD LIVER OIL DIET FOR ARTHRITICS

Several physicians have theorized that oil can lubricate joints and thereby bring relief. Accordingly, Charles A. Brusch, M.D. and Edward T. Johnson, M.D., of the Brusch Medical Center in Massachusetts, selected ninety-eight arthritics for a cod liver oil diet program. Reporting to the *Journal of the National Medical Association* (July 1959), the doctors offered these facts:

Ninety-two of the ninety-eight responded within two to twenty weeks on the program. Cholesterol levels either dropped or could be controlled even though the arthritics were permitted eggs, butter and cod liver oil. The doctors say that one diabetic patient was able to stop taking insulin on this diet. Blood pressure levels were comfortably lower in most of the patients.

The doctors had a special restriction — junk food. "There was complete curtailment of soft drinks, candy, cake, ice cream or any food made up of white sugar . . . . Those who felt that the sacrifice of coffee was too great were allowed black coffee — fifteen minutes before breakfast."

Here is the diet:

1. Water was drunk one hour before breakfast or half an hour before the evening meal.
2. The only liquid permitted with meals was milk served at room temperature or warm soup.
3. Cod liver oil, together with two tablespoons of fresh, strained orange juice or two tablespoons of cool milk (the mixture was shaken well in a screw-topped jar) was taken on a fasting stomach at least four, but preferably five or more, hours after the evening meal (before retiring), or one or more hours before breakfast upon arising and at least thirty minutes after water intake. (Diabetics or people with heart trouble took the oil only twice a week.)
4. Tablets, pills or any supplements could be taken with water upon arising, with milk or soup at mealtime or with milk or soup at any time.
5. No sugar or any food made with sugar.
6. No coffee except at breakfast.

The program helped correct faulty body chemistry and promote overall good health and arthritis relief. Within several months, many of the arthritics responded with marked reduction of pain and a general improvement in their condition.

In commenting on the reason for this nutritional healing, Dr. Brusch says, "We felt these (rapid) improvements were due primarily to the cod liver oil and the unusual arrangements for liquid intake.

"In our opinion, there is a difference between water taken per se and the water content taken in the form of fruits and vegetables. We agree that water is water, regardless of its source and that the digestive tract cannot tell the difference; *but their surface tensions are considerably different, tap water having the highest surface tension level and fruit and vegetable water content being of the low range of surface tension levels.*

"More important, however, one must remember that water delivered into the digestive tract from an apple or a carrot would take one to four hours, depending on the rate of digestion — if it or they were singular foods or combined in a meal. This water (from fruits and vegetables) would appear in the bloodstream at a very slow rate.

"On the other hand, a glass of water, taken on an empty stomach, as suggested in our paper, *would be delivered in the system in a matter of minutes, not hours.*"

Dr. Brusch feels that water has a beneficial kidney-washing action. "Water, taken upon arising, will literally 'flush the kidneys' — the urine at this time being frequently crystal clear in the second voiding. Water taken with or immediately after a meal was seldom found crystal clear in the first voiding after a meal. We found an unusual arrangement for water intake plays a significant role in many areas." The doctor also suggests whole cod liver oil for maximum effect.

Dr. Brusch emphasizes that the core of healing is in making the entire body whole. "It is the combination of several factors that we strive to coordinate." That is, if you restore balance and healthy metabolism, relief from arthritis should be possible. Dr. Brusch says this program, under supervision, helps relieve much arthritis. It would appear to be a worthwhile contribution to the search for a cure.

A NUTRITIONAL APPROACH TO ARTHRITIS HEALING

"No person who is in good nutritional health develops rheumatoid or osteoarthritis," reports

Robert Bingham, M.D. in the *Journal of Applied Nutrition* (Winter 1972). Dr. Bingham says that most arthritics show a history of poor diet; the arthritic also has nervous-tension symptoms, is overactive, has poor resistance to infection and a history of serious infectious and inflammatory ailments. Many an arthritic overeats, especially junk foods such as refined flour foods, sugary sweets and fats.

Dr. Bingham describes a typical osteoarthritic as being middle-aged, overweight, malnourished on a low-protein, low-vitamin, low-enzyme but high-carbohydrate diet for months to years prior to the emergence of arthritis. By correcting nutritional imbalance and general living habits, he believes that arthritis can be healed.

"Nutritionists know that nervous and mental and emotional stress interfere with appetite, digestion, absorption of food, choices of food, nutritional habits and dietary patterns," continues Dr. Bingham, who runs his clinic in Desert Hot Springs, California. "Emotional stress exerts a control on the glands of internal secretion, particularly the thyroid, adrenals and pituitary and they play an important role in bone and joint metabolism. Naturally, *any disturbance in the nervous and emotional function of a person produces biological changes which can affect the bones or joints*." A correct diet and improvement in emotional control can ease stress and shield against the onset of arthritis.

Dr. Bingham starts treatment by writing down foods that the arthritic likes, dislikes or has allergies toward and then notes his general health. Overweight patients are put on a low-fat program. Osteoarthritics are given protein, calcium, vitamin and mineral supplements.

Dr. Bingham prescribes supplements in the form of six bone meal tablets daily or six oyster shell tablets. He prescribes 1,000 units of vitamin D from a natural source such as halibut liver oil, together with 25,000 units daily of vitamin A.

Typical Nutritional Healing Program for Patients
(outlined by Dr. Bingham):

1. Bed rest for sixteen hours a day.
2. Increase water consumption to eight or more glasses daily.
3. Slowly reduce drug intake to levels that will cause no pain.
4. A high protein diet.
5. All possible foods eaten fresh, raw and in their natural state. Use a blender or grinder, if necessary.
6. Eliminate all tobacco, alcohol, refined carbohydrates and saturated fats.
7. Take prescribed supplements of vitamins, minerals and enzymes.

Dr. Bingham notes that most arthritics are deficient in protein and vitamin C. He prescribes three glasses daily of raw milk for protein and calcium. If raw milk is unavailable, use pasteurized. But he prefers raw milk as he feels it contains an anti-stiffness factor that is destroyed by pasteurization. He prescribes 2,000 milligrams of natural vitamin C daily.

"It is important," says Dr. Bingham, "to preserve the natural food intact, including proteins and amino acids which have not been damaged by heat, hormones and enzymes which have not been altered by cooking, drying, storage or preservation and vitamins in the highest biological efficiency . . . *the foods must be as fresh and ripe as possible, grown by organic methods, free of residues of poisonous pesticides and fertilizers and delivered and prepared in as natural and palatable a form as possible.*"

Dr. Bingham tells of patients who have showed considerable improvement on a supervised program such as his. Since the program is conducted individually, it is important to obtain medical supervision. But it is proof that nutrition and diet can lessen and, possibly, erase the symptoms and cause of arthritis.

A BASIC DIETARY PROGRAM FOR ARTHRITICS

An Orlando, Florida, physician who has healed many arthritics through individual treatment and a dietary program has prepared a regimen that is both healthful and pleasant. Leo V. Roy, M.D., offers these basics for arthritics:

Proteins: Every meal should contain a protein. One-fourth of the daily food intake should be protein. Best sources are fish, eggs, nuts, cheese and raw certified milk.

Meats: Use internal organs, rich in vitamins and minerals. Avoid all canned and processed meat foods. Fowl, lamb and steak are good.

Dairy Products: All kinds of cheese, natural and fermented, yogurt and natural buttermilk.

Raw vegetables: All, especially celery, cucumbers and carrots. Make salads using oils for dressing.

Cooked vegetables: Baked potatoes and brown rice are nutritious. Use raw bean sprouts and other sprouts. *Do not overcook any vegetable.* Steam, bake or broil; use as little water as possible.

Fruits: Especially apples, grapes, bananas or local varieties.

Juices: Fresh-squeezed or bottled grape juice — no sugar added. No tomatoes. No citrus fruits except as flavoring. A maximum of one teaspoon lemon juice for salad dressing.

Cereals: Fresh-ground combinations — wheat, rye, sesame seed, flax and millet. Do not boil. Soak fifteen to twenty minutes in hot water over a double boiler, or soak overnight and warm. Raw sunflower seeds, raisins or shredded coconut may be added before eating.

Bread: Use sparingly. Only stone-ground fresh whole wheat or rye.

Soups: Bouillon or consommé.

Acid drink: Where there is insufficient acid or where there are calcium deposits, use one tablespoon apple cider vinegar to a glass of water (with or without one teaspoon of honey) at least twice daily.

Sweets: Old-fashioned blackstrap molasses (unsulphured) and pure cane syrup from health food stores. Only one sweet daily, in small quantity.

Oils: Especially sesame, safflower and sunflower oil. All seeds and raw nuts.

Avoid all of the following:

Tea	White flour
Coffee	White sugar
Alcohol	All hydrogenated (hardened) fats
Canned food	Roasted nuts
Commercial cereals	*Stale* nuts
Processed food	*Stale* wheat germ
Canned meats	*Stale* wheat germ oil

Do not use:

Overcooked and reheated foods

Jams, jellies, syrups, ice cream, soft drinks, tobacco

Chemicals added to food — sweeteners, emulsifiers, thickeners, fluoridated water. *Read labels carefully.*

General guidelines: Eat as much fresh raw fruit, vegetables and protein as possible. Chew thoroughly so that saliva is mixed with food and better utilized. Eat slowly. Avoid large quantities.

Dr. Roy's program is designed to prevent and relieve arthritis. It shows there is no one single factor in combating arthritis. Rather, the entire body must be adjusted through corrective diet and then the healing process can begin.

CHAPTER 4.

HOW VITAMINS AFFECT METABOLISM

VITAMINS act as sparkplugs, setting off a chain reaction within the body that ensures a balanced metabolism. This, in turn, can bring relief from arthritis. Arthritis is not a single specific disease affecting only the joints, but a symptom indicating that something has gone wrong with the system as a whole. Balanced nutrition with emphasis upon vitamins can do much to correct metabolic errors or disturbances.

Are vitamins really important? They seem so tiny, so minute. However, we know their presence or absence can spell the difference between good and ill health. Let's take a closer look at vitamins and the effect they have on metabolism.

Vitamins are part of the chemical regulators of the activities of living organisms. They set off the act and process of metabolism. (Simply, metabolism refers to the absorption, buildup and breakdown, utilization, storage and excretion of certain substances.) Vitamins are found in nearly every one of the billions of living tissues and cells in the body. Vitamins are the necessary link in the chain of essential nutritive substances required for the harmonious regulation of the physiological processes of the body.

Vitamins are needed for growth and reproduction; to form antibodies to resist disease and infection; to aid in coagulation of the blood so wounds will heal; to build immunity; to form intercellular substances; to maintain strong teeth, bones, nervous tissue, skin and blood, and to build muscles. Vitamins also function as coenzymes for vital body chemical reactions concerned with food metabolism and assimilation.

"Vitamins are not only curative for their specific deficiency diseases," says Joseph Berg, M.D., in *Bridges' Dietetics for the Clinician*, "they are also necessary to maintain normal health and resistance to other diseases."

Dr. Berg cautions against a deficiency of just *one* vitamin. "It needs to be emphasized at this point that our bodies need, not single food elements by themselves, but a suitable assortment of all. When we say *all*, we mean *all*. If one single food element is missing from our diet, our bodies fail to get what they need. We suffer from malnutrition just as truly as if many items were missing.

"One can appear perfectly normal in looks and behavior and yet be the victim of mild cellular malnutrition, which may impair the activity of important functioning tissues and decrease one's bodily efficiency materially."

Basically, vitamins are grouped in two separate divisions:

Group One: The four known fat-soluble vitamins — A, D, E, K. These are dissolved and then stored in body fat. They are found in fat-containing foods such as meats, butter, oils, eggs, fish and, to some extent, fruits, vegetables, grains, seeds and nuts.

Group Two: The water-soluble vitamins — B-complex, C, P and other trace elements that have yet to be isolated and discovered. These vitamins will dissolve in a liquid environment. They are *not* stored in the body and are lost in perspiration and wastes.

Your body must have a balance of all vitamins in

order to enjoy a healthy metabolism and to both protect against arthritis and to promote its healing. Many doctors have found that vitamins can help this process.

B-COMPLEX VITAMINS

Pantothenic Acid

Hormones secreted by the adrenal glands (a pair of small glands lying against the upper ends of the kidneys) such as cortisone, control a tendency towards inflammation in arthritis. A team of English physicians have found that a deficiency of *pantothenic acid* (one of the B-complex vitamins) may predispose arthritis and even inhibit healing. Pantothenic acid alerts the adrenal glands to secrete more natural cortisone to act as a buffer against arthritic inflammation.

Reporting in *Lancet* (26 Oct. 1963), the doctors say that daily injections of pantothenic acid slowly raised blood pantothenic acid levels resulting in improvement in the general condition and in metabolism, in better mobility of stiffened joints and a fall in the sedimentation rate (accumulated toxins, wastes in the bloodstream). When the arthritics were deprived of sufficient pantothenic acid, their symptoms worsened. With this B-complex vitamin, however, they found relief.

Pantothenic acid has a key metabolic position: it induces slow biochemical processes which ensure protection against arthritis, protects the epithelium and promotes tissue regeneration, protein synthesis, antibody production and corticoid synthesis. Accordingly, it creates an anti-arthritic body environment.

Pantothenic acid is found in fresh fruits, vegetables, soybeans, nuts, egg yolk, dessicated liver (a good source), beef liver and brewer's yeast.

If pantothenic acid is to function as an "arthritis buffer," the body should have at least 107 micro-grains daily. So say doctors in *Medical World News* (7 Oct. 1966) after testing a group of patients with arthritis. The doctors report that arthritics have a lesser amount of the acid and that symptoms became more and more severe as the level of deficiency increased.

The doctors then injected pantothenic acid into their patients with the reported results that they could move about more easily, enjoyed freedom from typical symptoms and felt generally better. They suggest that maintenance of a high level of pantothenic acid will reduce arthritic symptoms.

NIACIN (Vitamin B3)

Dr. Roger J. Williams, in *Nutrition Against Disease*, tells of the uses of niacin, also known as vitamin B3, by William Kaufman, M.D., in treating arthritic patients. Dr. Kaufman found that increased amounts of niacin are helpful in arthritis.

Dr. Kaufman, it is reported, prescribed from 400 to 2,250 milligrams of niacin every twenty-four hours. (The amount prescribed was adjusted to the severity of the case.) He found great symptom improvement when niacin levels were raised within the bloodstream.

Dr. Williams comments, "These results can best be interpreted to mean that the cellular structures involved in the impaired joints were often limited with respect to their niacin supply, something that all the cells need, and that massive doses somehow get beneficial amounts of this one nutritional element to these cells."

Niacin is found in liver, kidney, eggs, dessicated liver and brewer's yeast. It has one peculiarity: a few minutes after taking it you may feel flushed and tingly, particularly in your face and fingers. This will go away in a few minutes and is no cause for alarm.

PYRIDOXINE (Vitamin B6)

Vitamin B6 is also helpful to an important degree, notes John M. Ellis, M.D., in *The Doctor Who Looked at Hands*. The doctor finds that supervised supplements of pyridoxine are most effective in "relieving the pain, stiffness and 'locking' of finger joints," and also lessen problems of parasthesia (numbness), nocturnal paralysis of the arm and nocturnal muscle cramps as well as arthritic pain in the shoulders, hips and knees.

Dr. Ellis usually prescribes about 50 milligrams of pyridoxine daily. He reports no undesirable side effects after using this vitamin for eight years. The doctor does not claim that pyridoxine will cure arthritis. Finger joints and some other body parts, however, will benefit with the use of this vitamin. Furthermore, pyridoxine may well be considered the "missing link" in the nutrition chain and help restore body metabolism, thus alleviating arthritic symptoms.

Pyridoxine can be found in muscle meats, liver, green and yellow leafy vegetables, whole-grain cereals, bran from cereal grains, dairy foods, blackstrap molasses, wheat germ and brewer's yeast.

VITAMIN C

Build up your capillary system and you should help your arthritis. This is where vitamin C comes in, according to many reports.

A team of physicians treated a number of arthritics with supervised doses of vitamin C. Writing in the *Journal of American Geriatrics* (June 1956), the physicians prescribed vitamin C in large amounts for their patients and reported that their discomfort was much relieved after a month or six weeks.

Vitamin C helps to rebuild the capillaries, the small blood vessels that crisscross all the body's tissues. Through the walls of these capillaries food and oxygen are transported to nourish the cells and wastes are removed. The doctors feel that a healthy capillary system restores good metabolism, thereby lessening arthritic distress.

A vitamin C deficiency may cause capillary breakdown in the joints and subsequent arthritic reactions. When the capillaries are strengthened, there is less susceptibility toward inflammation.

The doctors treating the arthritic patients reported in the journal that vitamin C was given in amounts ranging from 600 to 1,000 milligrams daily in divided doses. Gradually, the amount was reduced to 300 milligrams which was kept as a daily maintenance dose.

As a result, arthritic symptoms were remarkably reduced. Blood pressure in most patients became normal. There was greater resistance to colds. But when the vitamin was discontinued, arthritis symptoms returned. While taking vitamin C the patients had less fatigue, less discomfort in the joints and showed a general improvement.

W. J. McCormick, M.D., in the *Archives of Pediatrics* (April 1955) spotlights the value of vitamin C for alleviating arthritis. Dr. McCormick notes that all forms of arthritis have one thing in common: *the cartilage involved in joints and the connective tissue surrounding them disintegrate. Therefore, if this condition could be corrected, arthritis might very well vanish.*

Dr. McCormick feels that vitamin C could help correct this problem. He writes, "The most definitely established function of vitamin C is that of assisting in the formation of collagen for the maintenance of integrity and stability of the connective tissues generally, and this would include the bones, cartilages, muscles and fascular tissues.

"In a deficiency of vitamin C, instability and fragility of all such tissues is believed to be caused by the breakdown of intercellular cement substance (collagen), resulting in easy rupture of any and all of these connective tissues." The doctor is referring to the discs of the backbone, the ligaments and small sacs in the interior of the joints and the cartilage which helps in the movement of joints. He says that a vitamin C deficiency makes the joints vulnerable to an ailment such as arthritis.

Some back pain may have its origin in arthritis. Vitamin C can also ease this problem. James Greenwood, M.D., writing in *Medical Annals of D.C.* (33:274) relieved his own back pain and that of his patients by taking 1,000 milligrams of vitamin C daily. The relief of back discomfort and prevention of increasing arthritis may have occurred when the vitamin C produced collagen which was then used to maintain the structure of intervertebral discs.

When we recognize that capillary failure may predispose arthritis, we can appreciate the value of sufficient vitamin C as a way to strengthen capillaries and build a barrier against arthritis.

The aspirin habit depletes the body's storage of vitamin C, notes H. S. Loh, a scientist, in *Journal of Clinical Pharmacology* (November-December 1973). Aspirin blocks the absorption of vitamin C by the blood cells. Therefore, more vitamin C is needed if aspirin is taken continuously. It is also reported that a steroid drug used by arthritics, prednisolone, can cause skeletal damage unless large amounts of vitamin C are taken to counteract this risk.

Scientists reported to the *Journal of Nutrition* (March 1974) that residents of soft-water areas, whose home pipes are made of galvanized iron, ought to increase their vitamin C intake. Soft water is corrosive enough to dissolve toxic cadmium from galvanized pipes and can cause all kinds of problems in the body. To protect against metabolic disturbances, it is important to take enough vitamin C.

This valuable vitamin can be found in fruits such

as oranges, grapefruit, cantaloupe, strawberries, lemons and limes; in vegetables such as raw cabbage, green peppers, broccoli, kale, collards, turnip greens, mustard greens and brussels sprouts; and in the highest concentration of all, in rose hips.

VITAMIN D

In some situations, a strong skeletal structure is a protection against arthritis. Vitamin D, a bone strengthener, can help the body against arthritis.

"Bone is a living substance that depends on a constant supply of nutrients for the manufacture of osteoid matrix and its subsequent mineralization," says Ronald A. Barrett, D.D.S., in the *Journal of Periodontology* (March 1968).

"Under physiological conditions," says Dr. Barrett, "adult bone is constantly and equally being formed and destroyed. Hence, two major groups of mechanisms are operative . . ." These two mechanisms require vitamin D.

Basically, vitamin D is manufactured in the skin through the action of ultraviolet rays of the sun. But pollution, smog and prolonged indoor living deprive the skin of direct sunshine. Vitamin D therefore, must be obtained from foods or supplements. A deficiency of foods containing vitamin D may be a factor in arthritic conditions and related problems such as osteoporosis (thinning of the bone) and osteomalacia (adult rickets).

Vitamin D is especially important if an arthritic is taking medication. While steroid drugs reduce swelling and mask pain, they also make the bone fragile and so increase the extent of the arthritis.

In a talk before the Arthritis Foundation (as reported to *Medical World News*, 13 July 1973), Bevra Hahn, M.D., assistant professor of medicine at Washington University, said that vitamin D can *reverse* the process of bone resorption (dissolving) caused by steroid drugs. Vitamin D also facilitates the intestinal absorption of calcium blocked by the steroids. A deficiency of the vitamin often so weakens the spinal column that a healthy sneeze can break a few vertebrae!

Dr. Hahn says that steroid therapy causes overactivity of the parathyroid glands resulting in the loss of more trabecular bone (supporting strands of connective tissue) than cortical bone (long outer bone). Therefore, she recommends the use of vitamin D to correct trabecular bone loss.

In her experiments Dr. Hahn treated arthritic patients with a prescribed amount of 50,000 units of vitamin D orally, three times a week, over a period of thirteen weeks. Tests showed that nine out of ten of the arthritic patients showed an increase in trabecular bone density. This meant a stronger skeletal structure that could help bring about the healing of arthritis and protect against the side effects of steroid drug therapy.

Of course, large doses of vitamin D can be risky and this program was carefully supervised. But prescribed vitamin D does offer hope for strengthening arthritic bones.

Vitamin D can be found in various fish liver oils, butter and milk and dairy products.

VITAMIN E

Much has been written about the "new" vitamin, vitamin E. It is "new" in the sense that its varied usefulness has only recently been studied.

In reported situations, vitamin E, taken in amounts of 100 international units, three times daily before meals, helped alleviate a painful leg ailment known as *systremma* (whatever is twisted together).

Vitamin E appears to improve glycogen storage in the muscles and thereby reduce arthritic pain in the legs. (Glycogen is a form of stored glucose manufactured by the liver.)

Fibrositis has responded to vitamin E therapy.

According to C. L. Steinberg, M.D., physician-in-charge of the Arthritis Clinic of Rochester General Hospital (*Annals of the N.Y. Academy of Science*, October 1969), fibrositis was healed with the use of vitamin E.

Dr. Steinberg tells of treating 300 patients with fibrositis (inflammation of the white fibrous connective tissues that form muscle sheaths) by prescribing vitamin E. He writes that the fibrositis was healed in a majority of these patients. He urges the patient to continue taking a maintenance supply of vitamin E daily, even after the symptoms have disappeared.

Dr. Steinberg also treated rheumatic fever patients with vitamin E and reports that their conditions improved considerably.

Wheat germ oil, rich in vitamin E, conquers some arthritic disorders.

Morris Ant, M.D., of Kings County Hospital in Brooklyn, treated arthritic disorders as well as patients with muscular ailments by applying wheat germ oil directly on the painful spot.

Writing in *Industrial Medicine* (June 1946), Dr. Ant reports that he used a 55 percent ointment of wheat germ oil and a food supplement of wheat germ oil, along with a diet that was rich in vitamin E foods. He tells of treating twenty patients. Of these, four case histories are especially interesting and offer hope for successful treatment of arthritic disorders.

1. *Housewife.* Her hands were swollen and stiff; local application of wheat germ oil returned her hands to their normal condition.
2. *Physician.* Arthritis had attacked this physician in his knees and back. The swelling was so painful, he could not walk. He was given wheat germ oil locally and internally and was soon able to resume his practice.
3. *Elevator operator.* He suffered a serious fall

resulting in pain and stiff muscles in his chest and legs, along with bronchial disorders. After several months of local and internal wheat germ oil, he returned to work, free from arthritic symptoms, except for a slight occasional limp. His bronchial disorder and asthma cleared up.

4. *Clerk.* A fall against the sharp corner of a desk led to a long-standing pain over her ribs, so severe she could not sleep. Local and internal wheat germ oil relieved her of all symptoms within several months.

In a later article in the *Annals of the N. Y. Academy of Science*, Dr. Ant, together with Erwin DiCyan, write of using vitamin E in arthritic disorders. This time, they describe a three-way program:

1. Orally, by means of capsules.
2. Intramuscularly, by means of injection.
3. Locally, by means of an ointment.

More than one hundred patients were given vitamin E in this program. The doctors report general relief from arthritic pain, improvement or disappearance of physical symptoms and increased joint mobility.

To further correct any errors in metabolism and for maintenance, the doctors put the patients on a nutritional food program. For example, a tablespoon of wheat germ was taken at breakfast. Lunch included a quarter-head of lettuce with peanut oil dressing and one banana. Dinner called for lean beef, spinach and lettuce with peanut oil dressing. All of this increased the intake of vitamin E, which apparently improved the metabolism of the patients enough to free them from their symptoms.

When vitamin E is added to standard drug procedures for treating arthritis, healing is quicker. The need for powerful drugs decreases and they may be completely eliminated in time.

The following report was made through the

Japanese Rheumatism Society and appeared in *Modern Nutrition* (2:67). Drs. Takefumi Morotomi and Sadao Kira of the University of Medicine at Kyoto, Japan, conducted a study of fifty patients who were receiving a form of cortisone, with additional vitamin E (150 to 160 milligrams daily). Most of the patients were able to reduce the steroid from 30 milligrams to 9 milligrams or less within nine weeks, when the amount of vitamin E was increased.

The Japanese physicians tell of a twenty-nine-year-old housewife who suffered from arthritis of the elbows, arms, fingers and legs. She was given high steroid therapy and showed some improvement. When doctors wanted to reduce the dosage, they found that this made her arthritis so much worse that she could scarcely walk. They then added vitamin E *together* with a reduced steroid of just 3 milligrams. She is now active enough to enjoy folk dancing and bicycle riding.

Vitamin E has the ability to replace the steroids in varying amounts. Vitamin E will also stimulate blood circulation in the fingers and toes. The doctors add that many of their arthritic patients no longer had a "cold" feeling in their limbs when vitamin E supplemented steroids.

In *Medical World News* (9:66) two physicians laud vitamin E for its ability to help control the side effects of drugs given for arthritis. The physicians suggest that vitamin E be used in combination with steroids for treating arthritic patients.

Vitamin E stimulates circulation in the extremities and helps provide more youthful flexibility of the limbs. These doctors gave 150 to 600 milligrams a day to their arthritic patients, together with the steroid drug prednisolone. Gradually, they lowered the drug from 30 milligrams a day to 9 milligrams, by increasing the vitamin E.

Some of the arthritic patients could take a drug dosage as low as 3 milligrams a day. Vitamin E helped offset side effects and also ease arthritic symptoms despite the low medication. The doctors say that vitamin E increases both the arterial and venous blood flow and also decreases capillary fragility.

Vitamin E apparently curbs the formation of excess calcium in bones. In Germany some arthritics responded to vitamin E treatment and had "young joints" again. The German medical journal, *Therapiewoche* (3,1953), describes 50 patients who suffered from *epicondylitis*—a form of arthritis in which the rounded end of the bone becomes inflamed and calcium deposits accumulate. The doctors gave each patient from 300 to 600 milligrams of vitamin E daily, orally. Within eight days, pain vanished. In four weeks, formation of calcium deposits stopped.

Vitamin E can be found in fresh, unheated vegetable and seed oils, wheat germ oil, wheat germ, whole grain cereals and whole grain bread products and brewer's yeast. Vitamin E and vitamin C are known to support each other and increase their effectiveness when taken together.

While one tiny vitamin cannot immediately erase arthritis, it can become a part of the vital chain that controls metabolism and thereby restore better balance within the body. This may help the body gather the necessary ammunition to fight arthritis.

CHAPTER 5.

MINERALS: NATURE'S HEALERS

LITTLE-KNOWN but powerfully effective nutrients in the mineral family play an important role in healing arthritis.

A pioneer in the use of mineral therapy for arthritis, Melvin Page, D.D.S., author of *Degeneration Regeneration*, has found that many of his patients responded well to his recommendations.

Dr. Page says that the source of arthritic conditions is an *imbalance* in the calcium-phosphorus ratio of the blood: the ideal proportions in a blood test reading are a calcium level of 10 and a phosphorus level of 4. If these proportions alter for one reason or another, problems such as arthritis result.

The mineral balance is sensitive to maintain.

Emotional and physical stress can cause an excess as well as depletion. Dr. Page says that when minor aches and pains occur, there is a feeling of distress. This creates tension which can drain minerals from the body. By increasing mineral intake and correcting the calcium-phosphorus ratio, there is hope for protection against arthritis as well as possible healing, according to Dr. Page's experience with his patients.

Other conditions that may cause arthritis, Dr. Page says, include poor sleeping habits, bad posture and congested circulation. The menopause is one of the conditions that most frequently stimulate arthritic symptoms.

The delicate calcium-phosphorus balance is upset during this time. Glandular-hormonal changes aggravate any beginning arthritic condition. This accounts for the preponderance of arthritis among women during this stage in life, when no such symptoms were previously noticed.

Dr. Page also says that sugar disturbs the mineral balance and paves the way for arthritic infection, along with other ailments. When large amounts of sugar are eaten, the high sugar calories count displaces an equal amount of calories from foods that contain minerals the body needs. Sugar upsets the calcium-phosphorus level. When the effect has worn off, the reverse occurs and the phosphorus level rises rapidly while the calcium drops. It is this see-saw effect that makes the body vulnerable to arthritis.

Dr. V. H. Bagnall, an osteopathic physician and surgeon, shares the view that sugar is a culprit in the formation of arthritis. As reported to *Prevention* (May 1971), Dr. Bagnall says, "The first patient I ever treated nutritionally was a rather heavy woman who was brought into my office by worried friends. She was suffering severely from arthritis, her joints were painful and her condition was extremely uncomfortable." The patient said she had gone the drug route and wanted no more. Dr. Bagnall offered this simple program:

"Nutrition was the only chance she left me so I told her to eliminate white sugar altogether from her diet. I told her to make a list of everything she eats — including condiments — and if it contains sugar, to throw it out."

Three months later, the woman returned. She appeared to be much better. As she eliminated sugar, the pain from her arthritis seemed to disappear. But when she had eaten a dish of sugary ice cream, "the pain increased and she couldn't get out of bed." And so, on a sugar-free diet, according to Dr. Bagnall, the woman could also enjoy an arthritic-free life.

It is believed by other specialists that sugar upsets the mineral balance and aggravates arthritis flareup and onset. It is simple to "kick" the sugar habit and enjoy better health of body and mind.

Just as vitamin E and vitamin C work together, calcium taken with vitamin D is helpful in nourishing the bone structure. Your bones not only support your body but they also store calcium. Vitamin D regulates calcium from the time it enters the body. It maintains the balance of calcium between the plasma and bone and it influences production of calcitonin and the parathyroid hormone to maintain a good mineral balance.

Your body requires a constantly available supply of both calcium and phosphorus circulating in the bloodstream to build and strengthen the bones and to control the vital functions of every cell and tissue.

Should the concentration of calcium ions (electrically-charged molecules) in the blood plasma drop below required levels, then both muscle and nerve cells react spontaneously; the voluntary muscles go into painful contractions. This sets off an arthritic condition and trouble begins in the muscles and joints.

As a protection against this reaction, your body tries to provide a sufficient supply of calcium to the blood; it takes calcium out of the bones and later returns it. For all of these functions, vitamin D is needed. It is vitamin D that enables the body to borrow calcium from the bones to use in the bloodstream, and later to return it to the bones for storage. The combination of calcium and vitamin D is obviously very useful.

LUBRICATION FOR ARTHRITIC JOINTS

World-famous scientist, Dr. Roger J. Williams,

author of *Nutrition Against Disease*, notes that minerals with other nutrients such as protein work to lubricate the joints and help arthritis. Dr. Williams says,

"Many of the difficulties associated with arthritic diseases stem from what in popular terms we may call poor lubrication. Our joints and all other movable structures in our bodies must be lubricated, and the lubricant commonly used is called 'synovial fluid.' Although the form of this fluid differs somewhat, depending on whether it is found in joint cavities, tendon sheaths or in bursae all forms seem to have properties in common, regardless of location.

"Synovial fluid is viscous, mostly a dilute water solution of various minerals, but containing about 1 percent of mucinous protein (mucoprotein) that gives it lubricating properties.

"It is closely related to interstitial fluid and to lymph, which together make up 15 percent or more of the body weight.

"We cannot effectively drink synovial fluid or its equivalent to improve lubrication. The water in fluid, of course, comes from the water we drink, and the minerals are supplied by our food. But the effective mucoprotein, like other body proteins, must be produced in our bodies by living cells (in the synovial membranes) from raw materials furnished by food. *If any mineral, protein or vitamin is in deficient supply, or if the cells are poisoned by bacterial toxins or allergens, this can partially incapacitate the cells, and can lead to poor lubrication, with every movement accompanied by pain.*"

Dr. Williams emphasizes, "Since enlargement of bones near joints and mineral deposits in cartilage are associated with arthritic disease, it seems likely that mineral imbalances may be involved as well. In this case, mineral nutrition may be a key factor."

The doctor explains that the lubricating quality of

synovial fluid is influenced by the minerals it contains. "In some individuals, the arthritic condition may be largely due to an inappropriate mineral balance."

Magnesium is often suggested as important in building arthritis resistance. W. C. Kuzell, M.D., in *Annals of Review Medicine* (2:367, 373, 374) reports that in test subjects, a magnesium deficiency leads to arthritis formation. It is possible that magnesium may be important for nourishing the skeletal structure and guarding against arthritis.

Minerals really can help protect against arthritic infection. For instance, they are needed for the formation of protein. Minerals are used by the vagus nerve that controls the stomach's ability to function. Minerals influence muscle contraction and nerve response. Minerals control body liquids to permit nutrients to pass into the bloodstream and aid in blood coagulation.

Water balance in the body is maintained by minerals. They draw nourishing substances in and out of billions of tissues. They serve to keep blood and tissue fluid from being either too acid or too alkaline. The glands secrete hormones because of minerals. Your nervous system responds because minerals spark its function. Minerals also help protect against nervous irritation.

Within your system, minerals leave "ash" which is worked into the fabric of every single muscle cell and body tissue and in synovial fluid, needed to provide lubrication. Bones are also strengthened and formed by minerals such as calcium. When the body needs to neutralize poisonous substances, it combines minerals with cellular wastes, neutralizing them and preparing them for elimination. Were it not for minerals, waste products would accumulate in the body and create a toxic reaction that could be fatal.

Let's take a look at some of the more essential

minerals and see how they can give protection against arthritis.

Calcium

A constituent of bones and teeth, 99 percent of your body's calcium is found in the skeletal structure. The remainder of a scant 1 percent circulates in the soft body tissues and fluids. Calcium is needed for normal bone and tooth development, for blood clotting, for enzymatic action and for the regulation of fluid passage through walls of tissues and cells. Calcium is stored inside the ends of bones in long, needlelike crystals called trabeculae. When you are in a stress condition (a contributing factor to arthritis), your body draws calcium from these bones, usually from the spine and pelvic areas. This causes a weakness that could lead to a vertebrae fracture.

Calcium is found in dairy and milk products, yogurt, natural cheeses, green vegetables such as kale, broccoli, collards, and in bone meal, a concentrated form of calcium available as tablets or powder.

Phosphorus

Each body cell contains phosphorus. About 66 percent of phosphorus is found in the bones in the form of calcium phosphate while the balance occurs as organic and inorganic phosphate in soft tissues. Organic phosphate compounds aid in converting oxidative energy to cellular work.

Phosphorus is in all dairy products, yogurt, natural cheeses, poultry, fish, peas, grains, beans and nuts.

Iron

All of the billions of body tissues and muscle cells need iron to provide them with oxygen — the breath of life. Iron is a vital component of hemoglobin, the oxygen-carrying pigment of the red blood cells.

Iron is contained in liver, kidney, heart, egg yolk,

green leafy vegetables, dried fruits, molasses, cherries, raisins and grapes.

Iodine

This mineral is concentrated in the thyroid glands and present in the adrenal cortex, the lymph and also in the cerebro-spinal fluid. This makes iodine important in the maintenance of good skeletal health. Myoglobin (an iron substance resembling hemoglobin) combines with iodine to serve as a storage site for oxygen in muscular tissue.

Iodine is found in iodized salt, kelp, salmon, brown rice, beans, bananas and green leafy vegetables.

Sodium

A principal element in extracellular body fluids, sodium influences the osmotic pressure and fluid passage between blood and tissues, the acid-base body balance and the heartbeat. Sodium also influences other minerals in the blood to become more soluble and prevents them from clogging.

Sodium is in lean meats, fish, poultry, milk, cheese, beets, beet greens, Swiss chard, celery and carrots.

Potassium

This mineral works together with sodium in controlling body fluids and essential physiological and metabolic processes. Potassium is found mostly *inside* the cells while sodium is mostly *outside* the cells. To prevent a painful tug of war, these two minerals must be kept in balance.

Potassium is in dried apricots, beans, beets, raisins, avocados, bananas, barley, spinach, yeast, fish, poultry, milk and eggs.

Magnesium

Closely related to both calcium and phosphorus in its location, about 70 percent of magnesium in the body is in the bones. The remainder is in the soft tissues and blood.

Magnesium may be found in legumes, cereal grains, nuts, dairy foods, egg yolk, whole grain foods, citrus fruits, leafy vegetables, dates and figs.

Copper

A nutritional partner of iron, copper helps metabolize food into hemoglobin, the oxygen-carrying ingredient found in all red blood cells. This enrichment of the bloodstream helps maintain good health.

Copper is contained in beef and calf liver, almonds, apricots, black mission figs, loganberries, walnuts, egg yolk and blackstrap molasses.

Sulphur

This mineral helps build resistance to bacterial infections which so often precede arthritis, and also helps the liver absorb other minerals. It is a vital part of protein metabolism and body oxidative processes.

Sulphur is in cabbage, molasses, brussels sprouts, red currants, cranberries, pineapple, brazil nuts, and dried chestnuts.

Silicon

Found in muscles, connective tissue and cellular walls, silicon is a "sleeper" mineral, not well known. Its valuable function is as a partner to natural flourine in building strong bones.

Silicon is found in whole grain foods, lentils, mushrooms, liver, tomatoes, carrots, buckwheat products, and fresh fruits.

Zinc

Found in major body glands, zinc is important for the metabolism of carbohydrates and for helping foods become absorbed through the intestinal walls. Zinc also is valuable for regulating body metabolism, a key to combatting arthritis.

Zinc is contained in the green leaves of vegetables, egg yolk, seeds, nuts, peas, beans, organ meats and many fruits.

CHAPTER 6.

RELIEF WITH HOME THERAPIES

SEVERAL HOME THERAPIES have been reported that have helped sufferers from arthritis by adjusting the metabolism in the body and helping the system to function more smoothly.

BROMELAIN, THE PINEAPPLE ENZYME

A common, everyday fruit, the pineapple, has been found to reduce the inflammation that plagues the arthritic. The pineapple is not only delicious, but it is a source of vitamins A, B-complex, C and E. It also supplies such important minerals as calcium, phosphorus, iron, copper and magnesium and other helpful trace elements.

Most important, the fresh, uncooked pineapple is a source of a little-known enzyme called *bromelain*.

Enzymes are protein substances found in all living animal and plant matter. They are needed for building and rebuilding body tissues and cells. They aid in digestion of all foodstuffs, stimulate the flow of hormones, improve the bloodstream and influence all life processes. Enzymes are the catalysts that break down ingested food so that it can be absorbed into the bloodstream. Each enzyme acts on a specific type of food. Because heat destroys enzymes, it is important to eat plenty of raw plant foods.

Bromelain enzymes in raw pineapple have a

special healing characteristic. They reduce inflammation and edema (excessive accumulation of fluid) and protect against infection. Bromelain also helps dissolve accumulated fibrin deposits that are often a source of arthritic pain. According to M. G. Cirelli, M.D., in *Clinical Medicine* (June 1967), during the process of inflammation, fibrogen (a soluble blood plasma protein) is transformed into a soft and partially polymerized insoluble fibrin (a protein) in the walls and tissues of tiny blood vessels. (Polymerization is a reaction wherein small fibrin molecules combine to form larger and more complex molecules. These deposits of partially polymerized fibrin reduce the permeability of vessels and tissues and thereby obstruct the ability of edema fluid to return to circulation.)

Dr. Cirelli explains that pineapple "bromelains may act by depolymerizing these occlusive deposits, thereby restoring drainage and increasing permeability." We know that fibrin is an essential bloodclotting factor; we are told by Dr. Cirelli that bromelains do *not* disturb this natural process.

Over a five-year span, Dr. Cirelli treated about 700 patients with bromelains. Problems included inflammation, edema, related conditions such as bruises or contusions, abrasions, sprains, surgical wounds, boils, cellulitis (spreading inflammation of connective tissues) and various forms of ulcers. There was a successful healing rate for most of these problems.

"Therapy with bromelains for the condition indicated," says Dr. Cirelli, "was usually followed by a marked subsidence of pain, edema and inflammation. The increased mobility and decreased period of disability facilitated a quicker return to normal activities. The time between admission and discharge of patients treated with bromelains was estimated to have been reduced by 30 to 50 percent. No toxic effects attributable to the medication were observed."

Dr. Cirelli reports that in many situations, the use of bromelains made it unnecessary to use other therapies such as splints, immobilizing devices and bandages, heat, debridement (removal of devitalized tissue from a wound) or compresses.

Drs. Abraham Cohen and Joel Goldman, reporting to the *Pennsylvania Medical Journal* (June 1964), tell of treating twenty-nine patients troubled with rheumatoid and other forms of arthritis. The doctors decided to use bromelain enzymes for the residual soft tissue inflammation often accompanying joint involvement in arthritis. In 72.4 percent of the cases, swelling was diminished and pain relieved.

The doctors are quick to say that bromelains should not be considered a substitute for drugs. Quite often, they will use cortisone and steroids in very low amounts; and they do concede that drugs have their place in treatment. But frequently, the doctors report, soft tissue swelling becomes painful and restricts free movement. The pain continues after the joint itself is no longer in an active inflammatory state.

This is because the fluid has been trapped in the adjoining tissue and causes pain. Therefore, they use bromelain enzymes to help depolymerize these fluid deposits; the enzymes help restore better fluid drainage, which in turn reduces discomfort and inflammation.

Drs. Cohen and Goldman write about a thirty-six-year-old woman troubled with a quiescent (mild symptomatic) rheumatoid arthritis. They saw that she had a residual swelling around her right knee. A short time after bromelain therapy was given, the swelling was reduced from 45 centimeters in circumference to 39 centimeters. The doctors say, "There was a return of some of the swelling when bromelains were stopped, which disappeared when bromelains were again administered."

The doctors also tell of treating a thirty-four-year-old woman with steroid drugs for active joint involvement in fingers and wrist. The swelling did not go down until they used bromelains as well.

It is believed by many specialists that bromelain therapy works because some portion of the enzyme gets through to the site of inflammation and there soothes the pain. Bromelains help the proteolytic (protein digesting) action in the system which improves the general metabolism so vital for healing arthritis.

It is simple to relieve your arthritic discomfort with pineapple freshly sliced for a snack or dessert or drink a glass or two of fresh pineapple juice whenever you like.

HEALING WITH HELIOTHERAPY

Warm weather, sunshine and heat from many sources can have a palliative effect upon arthritic pain. Even white light can be helpful. But it has been found that fluorescent lights create an adverse reaction. The flickering light of typical fluorescent bulbs can upset the body's metabolism and rate of assimilation and predispose it to many disturbances. Artificial light offers a spectrum that is different from sunlight and may reduce resistance to arthritis and other ailments.

Dr. Richard Wurtman of the Massachusetts Institute of Technology, writing in the *New England Journal of Medicine* (12 Feb. 1970) tells us, " 'Daylight' fluorescent bulbs provide very little long-wave ultraviolet light and emit yellow and red radiations in a ratio quite different from that present in sunlight. Prolonged exposure to this unplanned phototherapy might have physiological consequences . . . whether we like it or not, light is another thing that physicians must now worry about."

Because faulty calcium absorption often precedes

arthritis, it is important to note that a healthier type of light improves its absorption and therefore is a beneficial influence on arthritis.

Dr. Wurtman reports that when the body is exposed to a natural form of light (such as sunlight or incandescent bulb) whose emissions duplicate the solar spectrum, the intestinal absorption of calcium in healthy people is improved. Natural light bulbs (available at many hardware stores) give off small amounts of long-wave ultraviolet light and the additional vitamin D helps the body absorb calcium. Accordingly, this offers hope for diminishing the symptoms related to faulty calcium metabolism.

John Ott, Ph.D., a light researcher and founder of the Environmental Health and Light Research Institute and author of *My Ivory Cellar*, feels that many ailments can be improved with natural heliotherapy from sunlight.

Dr. Ott himself says he had arthritis but after six months of conscious exposure to natural sunlight, he began to improve. "Suddenly, I didn't seem to need the cane . . . . My hip hadn't felt this well for three or four years. I began walking back and forth a mile. I ran into the house, up stairs two at a time, to tell my wife." He tells of friends who used heliotherapy and were relieved of more than just their arthritis and bursitis, but also recovered from ulcers, acne, bleeding gums and even hay fever.

To reduce your arthritic pain, try to spend as much time as possible outdoors. Dr. Ott suggests avoiding sunglasses since the light energy in sunshine hits your retina, stimulates the pituitary gland and improves your condition. Of course, avoid looking directly at the sun.

ULTRASOUND THERAPY TO LOOSEN JOINTS

It looks no larger than a breadbox and consists of only a few gauges, dials and gadgets. There are cords running from it, and a spray nozzle device about the size of your palm. But it does not spray water. Instead, the machine sends out what is known as ultrasound or sound waves that travel at such a high frequency they cannot be heard by the human ear. But they can be *felt* by the body. This is its purpose.

When the ultrasound therapy device is used, the part of the body to be treated is first coated with gel. Then a transducer (power-activating device) is placed against the injured area. The gel is to keep the sound waves from being lost in the air (which does not transmit them) and to carry the waves directly to the skin.

In the hands of a qualified physical therapist, the ultrasound machine is adjusted to emit a prescribed power or intensity of sound waves. The typical frequency for arthritic joint stiffness may be from 800,000 to 1,000,000 cycles per second, 40 times higher than the 20,000 cycles per second which are within normal hearing range. To raise the sound wave intensity, the therapist turns a dial, much as you would adjust the volume on a record player. In a few seconds the carefully regulated frequency can soothe or deaden pain and simulate the feel of a gentle massage. This brings great relief to arthritics.

As early as September 1965, ultrasound therapy helped arthritics, as reported to the *Journal of the American Physical Therapy Association* by John L. Echternach, M.S. Two of his cases indicate the capacity of ultrasound:

At age fifty-eight, one man had such shoulder pain that he could hardly make the slightest move without a reaction. He was unable to work. After one month of ultrasound therapy, the shoulder pain was gone, he recovered an almost normal range of motion and could return to work.

At age forty-seven, one man was troubled with calcific shoulder tendonitis. In this condition, calcium forms along a tendon, creating such irritation that the tendon cannot stretch fully. Initially, he was treated with hot packs and exercise but these proved to have little effect. After about twelve ultrasound treatments, he had very little pain and normal flexion. An X ray showed that the calcification had disappeared.

Echternach states that close to nine out of every ten patients showed good results through ultrasound therapy. About six out of every ten bursitis victims also showed improvement. "Patients were considered to demonstrate good results if they exhibited normal range of motion (equal to the uninvolved shoulder), had minimal or no pain and were able to return to full duties at work." According to Echternach, this suggests that "a trial of ultrasound therapy would be indicated in both acute and chronic phases of shoulder disability."

Physical Therapy (April 1970) describes a group of patients troubled with chronic arthritis. James E. Griffin, Ph.D., and his colleagues treated some 120 patients (from age twenty-eight to seventy-three with most over fifty) troubled with osteoarthritis or similar joint diseases affecting the shoulder, spine, hip, thoracic or lumbar (lower) vertebrae or knee, etc. In treating these patients, Dr. Griffin gave them ultrasonic therapy in varying degrees. He found that *lower* frequencies were more effective. Says Griffin: "The superior pain-relieving effects of low-frequency ultrasound in shoulder, vertebral, hip and knee lesions are assumed to be the result of the greater depth of penetration of this frequency."

HEALING BENEFITS OF ULTRASOUND
When a physical therapist offers drugless ultrasound healing, there are three basic benefits:
1. Penetrating waves soothe acute arthritic pains and are reportedly safer than potentially dangerous corticosteroid drugs. Furthermore, it is reported that when an ultrasonic device

drives corticosteroid ointment through the tissue to the injury site, there is much more benefit. It is also hoped that ultrasound will reduce the amount of required oral corticosteroids, thus limiting their side effects.

2. Ultrasound produces normal heat as the sound waves rub against cell molecules and cause them to vibrate. Ordinary heat packs, infrared and other methods are helpful but limited since they cannot penetrate to any appreciable degree beneath the skin. Ultrasound is able to penetrate the joint, where needed, for increased warmth and healing heat.

   (Heat is important for relief of arthritic pain because it increases metabolism, speeds production of natural joint lubricants, reduces swelling, helps break down undesirable and painful calcium formations and increases the blood supply. It is an important therapy for arthritis.)

3. Ultrasound provides a natural and deep massage to the painful tissue; it relaxes spasm-twisted muscles that are causing pain to ligaments and tendons. The sound waves also unwind muscles constricting blood vessels; this stimulates a healthy blood flow and soothes pain. The massage effect of ultrasound also helps to depolymerize (soften and liquify the cementlike substance in long-chained protein molecules), so that tissues can have more flexibility. Therefore, by relaxing muscles and tendons that are spasmodic and painful, motion is possible, and the limb can flex again.

Since ultrasound is a comparatively new method of natural healing, it should be used with care. There are still some drawbacks — specifically, limits as to the amount of intensity and frequency that the arthritic part can endure; also, there are limits to the duration of heat the limbs can take. Public and governmental standards need to be established. The calibrations, outputs and intensities have to be regulated. More knowledge is needed. At the present time, however, ultrasound is beneficial and should be considered as a natural way to promote healing and reduce the need for drugs.

To help the entire body resist arthritis, natural programs should be considered. When errors in metabolism are corrected through the use of these methods, there is hope for combatting the disease.

CHAPTER 7.

GOUT: A NUTRITIONAL APPROACH

GOUT is best (and unpleasantly) known for its periodic and sudden occurrence, bringing severe pain and swelling to certain joints, especially the big toe.

What Is Gout? A metabolic ailment striking the joints and kidneys in which the body metabolism is upset; gout is characterized by the presence of more uric acid in body tissues than nature intended. In a very serious metabolic upset, crystals of monosodium (a uric acid salt) form in one or more joints. This causes extreme pain and inflammation.

What Is Uric Acid? A substance made in the body as part of the normal life process, uric acid is manufactured from substances called purines in a series of various metabolic reactions. Normally, uric acid is discharged through the waste channels of the body. At times, however, the body stores an excess of uric acid in the bloodstream, thus precipitating an arthritic gout attack.

How Much Uric Acid Should the Body Have? In a healthy person, the blood and tissue fluid concentration will remain at about .02 percent; any excess is passed. The solubility of uric acid is about .06 percent. Above this level, acid salt crystals may form and gout develops.

Why Do Uric Acid Levels Rise Above Normal? The diet may be too high in purine-containing foods.

Metabolic defects within the system may over-produce uric acid. Too little may be excreted through the kidneys.

What Are Other Causes of Gout? There are metabolic disorders of the bone marrow known as polycythemia vera or leukemia; these can increase production of uric acid. Often, drugs may cause a reaction that induces gout. One such drug is chlorothiazide, a diuretic (water-passing) medication.

Who Develops Gout and at What Age? More men than women develop gout since they have higher average uric acid levels in the blood; it usually strikes after middle age in both sexes.

Where Does Gout Frequently Strike? Usually, the big toe is the victim. This toe receives the most pressure per square inch on its joint during walking than any other part of the foot. This constant strain may make it vulnerable to gout as well as osteoarthritis.

Why Is Gout So Painful? Basically, because there is severe inflammation and swelling of the sensitive nerve endings in the joint space. Swelling is caused by an accumulation of fluids from the blood vessels in the affected region. During inflammation, blood vessels turn porous. Therefore, an inflamed joint contains much more blood than a normal joint. This creates a feeling of excessive warmth and gives the skin the reddish-purple tinge characteristic of gout. Reduce the inflammation and swelling and the pain is eased.

What Drugs Are Available for Gout? A number of drugs are used; most, however, have unpleasant side effects. *Colchicine* is very powerful and may cause diarrhea and stomach cramps as well as considerable discomfort. *Phenylbutazone* may cause stomach upset, sore throat and skin outbreak and can only be endured for short periods of time. *Indomethacin* must be used for short periods, for it causes upset stomach, a feeling of light-headedness and headache. Other drugs are available; most have health risks.

What Can Be Done to Ease Gout? Here is a two-step program to try: (1) Rest the aching joint. If in severe pain, remain in bed. Avoid putting weight on the joint until the ache is gone. Avoid any undue strain (or injury) on the affected joint even after the attack has passed. (2) Drink lots of liquids—water, fruit and vegetable juices, herb teas, coffee substitutes such as Postum—as many beverages as possible. Increased liquid intake washes excess uric acid from your system and guards against kidney stone formation.

Can a Corrective Diet Be Helpful? Yes. Since each case of gout (and arthritis, in general) is unique, it is important to follow your doctor's diet suggestions and other advice. A general rule is to eliminate the following high-purine foods which produce uric acid: sweetbreads, anchovies, sardines, liver, kidney, meat extract, alcohol, pork, heavy gravies; *limit* spices and seasonings of all types.

Medium-purine foods include lean meats, fish, peas, beans, lentils, asparagus, cauliflower, spinach, mushrooms. Eat them more liberally, with your doctor's permission. Foods low in purine may be eaten almost without restriction, if your doctor agrees. Acceptable foods are vegetables (except those listed above), all fruits, milk, cheese, eggs, yogurt, dairy products, cereals (except whole wheat), nuts and seeds.

In preparing a diet, note that a *high-carbohydrate diet* increases uric acid secretion in some. A *high-fat* diet retards uric acid secretion in some but may result in a higher secretion in others. It is a good idea to limit both of these nutrients as well as high-calorie foods.

Is a Cherry Diet Helpful for Gout Control? There has been some research in this field, pioneered by

Doctor Ludwig W. Blau. In *Texas Reports On Biology And Medicine* (Vol. 8, Fall 1950), Dr. Blau writes that twelve cases of gout responded favorably when the patients ate about one-half pound of fresh or canned cherries per day. These could be sour, black, Queen Anne or black Bing cherries. In one case, only the juice was taken and this was equally as effective in reducing the acid levels.

Others have also found that cherries are helpful. It is believed that their pigment contains a high amount of malic acid, citric acid and other substances that appear to influence the quantity of uric acid in the bloodstream. It is a natural method worth exploring if it can bring you relief.

Since gout is often traced to a metabolic imbalance within the system, correction of this error can result in an alleviation of the condition. With proper care, recurrent gout attacks may be eliminated, or at least reduced in frequency and severity.

With natural methods the chances of being crippled by gout may be almost non-existent.

CHAPTER 8.
FOOT CARE AND COMFORT

THE JOINTS that are affected most frequently by arthritis are in the hands and feet. Although it is well known that the disease strikes the hands, arthritic conditions in the feet are often not recognized as such or are disregarded.

In foot arthritis there is a serious erosion of the joint cartilage and excessive growth of bone around the joint. While such changes produce little pain, they do restrict free movement.

Constant pulling of joint ligaments in an imbalanced foot results in repeated inflammation at the edges of the joint surface. These soon become irregular in appearance. At times, the pulling of tendons and larger ligaments can be so intense, there is a drawing away of the bone from the normal outline; this forms a bony outgrowth or *osteophyte*.

Center foot joints are the first to react. When the metatarsal and toe joints are affected, there is more serious dislocation of the toes. This upsets the natural foot balance and the situation becomes worse. Often, a chain reaction results and arthritis flares up more seriously in other parts of the body.

Knee arthritis can be caused by poor foot posture. Body imbalance with weight pushed to the inner side of the foot makes the leg turn in a degree of genuvalgum, or knock-knee. This unnatural and unhealthy pressure causes tension against the soft tissues and arthritic pain is felt in the knees. For pain to be reduced, the strain to the knee must be relieved through proper podiatric and/or medical care and better-fitting footwear.

The hips may be affected, too. When feet are imbalanced, there is limited movement in the hip joints; the body is inclined to a strained, waddling gait and that throws the entire skeleton out of kilter and causes symptoms of hip arthritis. Eventually, weight is thrown on the inner side of the foot and the hip joint is unable to move in a full inward rotation. If untreated, there may be degenerative changes and the hip joints may be seriously damaged.

Foot arthritis may also cause head-neck distress. Whether in the foot, knee or hip, foot arthritis may force the head and neck to bend forward during walking. Holding the head and neck in this unnatural position can cause a partial dislocation between the spinal vertebrae of the neck. Thus painful feet and poor posture may throw the entire body out of line.

FOOT CARE BEGINS WITH COMFORTABLE SHOES

Your feet will feel better in comfortable shoes. The Arthritis Foundation says, "wearing 'fashionable' shoes which squeeze the toes together often causes severe deformity and disability of the feet. In addition, it makes it difficult to maintain correct posture.

"A properly fitting oxford shoe with a 'straight last' is usually prescribed by the doctor, for both men and women. *For ordinary daily wear, your shoes should have heels that are low and wide.*

"Your doctor may recommend certain additions to your shoes. For example, perhaps you need a long counter or Thomas heel, which prevents the feet from rolling inwards; or a metatarsal bar to relieve pressure on the ball of the foot; or wedges to prevent inward turning of the feet. Such shoes are available in many shoe stores and need not be made to order."

When you buy shoes, keep these pointers in mind:

1. The shoe should be a half-inch longer than your foot.
2. Make sure the sole is as wide as your foot, with the widest part at the second joint of the big toe.
3. The shoe should have enough toe room so that your toes can move freely when walking.
4. A snug fit at the heel and instep is important.
5. There should be a soft, supple upper of leather or fabric.

Unfortunately, foot-flattering heels don't always conform to good shoe rules. A woman wearing them is in a constant battle to compensate for her tilted position. This takes nervous and muscular energy and is quite tiring. It may also lead to arthritis.

High heels may be fine for dress. But try to wear lower, broad-heeled shoes for all other activities, including housework. Remember, too, that varying your heel heights will keep the muscles in your ankles and legs strong and healthy. Many women who wear high heels for several years suffer from sharp pains in their calves when they change to lower shoes. Steady wearing of high-heeled shoes tends to shorten the calf muscles and causes arthritic-like pain. Avoid these styles if possible, but if you must wear them, do so for short periods of time.

KEEPING FEET HEALTHY

Here are some general rules for better foot care and for relieving arthritic foot discomfort:

1. Keep your feet clean. Wash them once a day, using a mild soap and warm (not hot) water. Apply lanolin, olive oil, bland creams or lotions to dry skin. Dry feet thoroughly; blot, do not rub hard, with a towel. Use a foot powder.
2. Trim your toenails. Cut them evenly and not too

close to the flesh.

3. Change your shoes often. If possible, alternate footwear so the same pair is not worn two days in a row. This allows them to dry out and air. They'll wear and feel better. Change socks and stockings at least once a day.

4. A mist of podiatrist-approved foot spray, applied to your feet and the insides of your shoes each morning will help your feet stay cool and fresh. Tuck a purse-size container of foot spray in your handbag or pocket to help soothe hot, tired feet on shopping trips or when travelling.

5. Massage is a wonderful pick-me-up for tired feet and legs. Smooth on a cooling cream (ordinary hand lotion is good) with a kneading, rotating motion, working from heel to knee. Massage each toe and gently tug it outward.

6. Whenever possible, expose your feet to sun and air. Athlete's foot thrives on heat, moisture and darkness, so a foot that's always in a shoe is especially prone to such infections.

7. Make sure your shoes fit with no uncomfortable binding or pinching. Check them frequently for runover heels and broken-down shanks. Not only are they unattractive, but both conditions indicate a weakness in the feet which can and should be corrected.

8. Exercise your feet. Keep them limber by wiggling your toes and by raising yourself on your tiptoes regularly.

9. Keep feet warm and dry. Be careful of exposing them unnecessarily to cold and dampness. Never let them remain wet (or even damp from perspiration) longer than is absolutely necessary.

10. Do not use tight garters or anything that will constrict circulation.

11. Avoid using harsh medication such as antiseptics containing iodine or carbolic acid, corn

cures or chemical compounds and ointments for athlete's foot.

12. Wear rubbers or boots when working in wet or damp surroundings. Men should wear heavy woolen socks or two pairs of cotton socks under such conditions. Women should use foot coverings under their hose or wear cotton socks over them.

13. Itching, blisters, cracking, weeping or sores that do not heal are signs that something is wrong. See your podiatrist and/or physician.

KEEPING FEET CLEAN

Next to properly fitting footwear, the most effective way to ensure foot health is to keep feet as clean as possible. There are more pores to the square inch on the soles of the feet than anywhere else on the body. Moreover, the feet get less air than most other parts of the body and pick up dust and dirt more easily.

Bathe your feet in warm, soapy water at least once a day. Scrub vigorously between the toes and at the heels, preferably with a pedicure brush, and then dry your feet carefully.

Foot powder is as important as bath powder and other body fresheners. Use it generously after a bath and several times daily, both on your feet and in your shoes. This helps keep feet dry by absorbing excessive perspiration.

After every bath, check for blemishes or rough skin areas. If they're tended to immediately, you'll avoid more serious foot troubles later.

If a corn is forming, apply a cushioned protective pad to reduce further pressure from shoes. If the skin at the heel or ball of the foot is rough and dry, use a pumice stone specially contoured for use on the foot.

EXERCISES FOR TIGHT FEET

Congestion in the feet can be relieved with these easy exercises:

1. Sit on the floor with the feet pointing straight ahead. Curl toes under and, with heels on floor, turn feet inward. Hold for count of two; relax. Repeat ten times.

2. Walk around barefoot on tiptoe and stretch up. Remember to do this daily. Follow a regular route—from wash basin to bed at night, for example.

3. Barefoot, try picking up marbles or a pencil with your toes. This also helps limber up the arch.

4. Walk alternately on the inner and outer edges of the feet, keeping your soles off the floor as much as possible.

5. After bathing, stand on one end of a towel and try to "rake" the rest of it in with your toes.

HOME REMEDIES FOR FOOT COMFORT

Here are several time-tested folk healers to help your feet look and feel better:

Dusting Powder. Mix 2 teaspoons baking soda and 5 tablespoons talcum powder in a shaker-top container. Use as a foot dusting powder daily and after a bath.

Foot Ache Mix. Dissolve in 2 quarts of lukewarm water 2 teaspoons Epsom salts, 1/2 teaspoon boric acid, 2/3 teaspoon powdered alum and 4 pinches menthol crystals. Stir well with your hand. When fully blended, use as a foot soak to ease aches and pains.

Sand Walk. Fill a dishpan with sand and moisten slightly. Then "walk" in the sand, digging in with the toes and heels. This helps keep your soles soft and provides good exercise, similar to walking barefoot on a wet beach.

Contrast Bath. Soak feet in hot water and dissolved salt for two minutes. Then switch to a cold water (no salt) soak for two minutes. Repeat five times. Finish with cold water, blot dry, splash with cologne or dust with powder. In a hurry? Hold feet under hot-as-you-can-comfortably-stand running water; switch to cold. Repeat several times. Finish with cold wash, then cologne or powder. This relieves aches and encourages better circulation.

Foot Soak. Keeping your feet in plain warm water for five minutes and toweling briskly afterwards will produce a tingling sensation that indicates the blood is flowing freely. It helps the health and flexibility of your feet and legs, too.

CHAPTER 9.

EVERYDAY HINTS FOR BETTER LIVING

A FEW simple adjustments in your daily activities and way of life can lessen the problems of arthritis. Here are some suggestions that will enable you to combat arthritic stiffness and discomfort.

CORRECTING FAULTY POSTURE

When you walk, sit, stand and work with good posture, your entire body feels better and is protected against arthritic pain. Basically, body strain through faulty posture or carrying heavy loads brings on weakness that results in loss of muscle power and puts the entire body out of alignment and makes it more susceptible to arthritic pain.

Start with correct posture. Hold your head high, keep your shoulders straight, your stomach in and hips and knees straight. Do *not* slump. This simple but healthy stance takes pressure off your joints and distributes it evenly throughout your body. It also helps you balance easily on your feet.

When you walk, let your arms swing freely at your sides. Shift your weight gently from one side to the other. Try not to carry packages. Heavy weights strain and fatigue those muscle groups already over-burdened by arthritis. If you must carry something, use both arms.

Basically, good sitting posture calls for a straight-back chair with a firm seat. Keep your head up and shoulders straight, your stomach in and both feet flat on the floor. Sit whenever you can but take care not to become too sedentary since joints must be kept mobile and activity is important for correct metabolism. When you do sit, select a chair with arm rests. Be sure to maintain good sitting posture all the time. To help your back recover from arthritis, always give it good support. Avoid sitting on easy or soft chairs, the edges of tables, desks or beds and couches with rounded contours.

Observe the rules of good posture even when stretched out in bed for relaxing or sleeping. Many serious arthritic deformities are traced to prolonged bedrest with poor (but "comfortable") posture.

Your mattress should be hard. Insert a one-half-inch-thick plywood board between the mattress and bedspring to avoid sag. This gives firm support to your back. The height of the bed should be comfortable for you to get on and off. If too low, insert blocks beneath the legs to raise it. If too high, ask your bedding store about a lower structure.

When in bed, either for sleeping or resting, train yourself to lie flat on your back in a straight position. Support your head with a small cushion. Do *not* support your knees with a cushion because this can make them stiff and bent. When lying in bed, keep your knees and head straight, your arms and hands extended at your sides. For back arthritis, you may choose to lie on your side to be more comfortable but *never* lie on your stomach.

Exercises for Arthritis Relief

Properly performed exercises will lessen arthritic pain, strengthen muscles and keep your joints in good condition. In the following simple exercises, it is important to avoid strain. Do them slowly. Choose a definite time for your basic exercises every day and stay on schedule.

Set aside about thirty minutes for a planned

program of physical activity. Several short periods of exercise may be more comfortable than one long period. Frequent exercise guards against stiffening of your joints.

Begin slowly. Gradually, increase the exercise time each day. If you feel any discomfort, stop. The goal is a gradual improvement of joint function. If your joints are inflamed or painful, keep motion to a minimum. Never strain yourself. Do the exercises gently and your arms and legs will feel supple, your entire body more flexible.

Wear comfortable clothes only; avoid tight-fitting or restrictive garments. If you feel better wearing foundation garments, do so. Shorts or slacks, T-shirts or short-sleeved blouses are best. Select well-fitting shoes with non-slip soles and low (or no) heels.

Walk

Starting Position: Stand erect, balanced on the balls of the feet.

Action: Begin walking briskly on a level terrain, preferably outdoors; walking around the room will do, if necessary.

Time: About two or three minutes.

Benefits: A good warm-up exercise; loosens muscles and prepares you for a full exercise schedule.

Alternate Walk-Jog

Starting Position: Same as for walking with arms held flexed and forearms parallel to the ground.

Action: Jogging is a form of slow running. First walk for fifty steps, then shift to a slow run with easy strides, landing lightly each time on the heel of your foot before transferring your weight to the whole foot. (This heel-toe running is the reverse of the sprint in which the runner stays on the balls of his feet.) Arms should move loosely and freely from the shoulders in opposition to the legs. Breathing should be deep but not labored.

Time: Alternately walk fifty steps and jog fifty steps for about three minutes.

Benefits: A warm-up for more advanced exercises; aids legs and circulation.

Bend and Stretch

Starting Position: Stand erect with feet shoulder-width apart.

Action: Count 1. Bend trunk forward and down, flexing the knees. Stretch gently and attempt to touch fingers to toes or floor. Count 2. Return to starting position. NOTE: Do this slowly; stretch and relax at intervals rather than in rhythm.

Time: Five to ten times.

Benefits: Loosens and stretches most muscles of the body; relaxes; a warm-up for more vigorous exercise.

Head Rotation

Starting Position: Stand erect with feet shoulder-width apart; place hands on hips.

Action: Count 1. Slowly rotate the head in a full circle from left to right. Count 2. Slowly rotate the head in the opposite direction. NOTE: Use slow motion; close eyes to avoid losing your balance or getting dizzy.

Time: Five to ten times in each direction.

Benefits: Loosens and relaxes muscles of the neck; firms throat and chin line.

Body Bender

Starting Position: Stand with feet shoulder-width apart; extend hands overhead, fingertips touching.

Action: Count 1. Bend trunk slowly to the left as far as possible, keeping hands together and arms and elbows straight. Count 2. Return to starting position. Counts 3 and 4. Repeat exercise to the right.

Time: Repeat five to ten times.

Benefits: Stretches arm, trunk and leg muscles.

Wall Press

Starting Position: Stand erect, head straight, back

against the wall and heels about three inches from the wall.

Action: Count 1. Pull in your abdominal muscles and press the small of the back tight against the wall. Hold for six seconds. Count 2. Relax and return to starting position. NOTE: Keep your entire back in contact with the wall on Count 1 and do not tilt your head backward.

Time: Repeat five times.

Benefits: Promotes good body alignment and posture; strengthens abdominal muscles.

Arm Circles

Starting Position: Stand erect with arms extended to the sides at shoulder height, palms up.

Action: Count 1. Make small backward circles with the hands. Keep head erect. Count 2. Reverse, turn palms down and do forward circles.

Time: Repeat five to ten times each way.

Benefits: Keeps shoulder joints flexible; strengthens shoulder muscles.

Half Knee Bend

Starting Position: Stand erect, hands on hips.

Action: Count 1. Bend knees halfway while extending arms forward, palms down. Keep heels on floor. Count 2. Return to starting position.

Time: Repeat five to ten times.

Benefits: Firms and stretches front leg muscles; improves balance.

Wing Stretcher

Starting Position: Stand erect, bend arms in front of chest with elbows at shoulder height, extended fingertips touching.

Action: Counts 1, 2, 3. Pull elbows as far back as possible, keeping arms at shoulder height. Return to starting position. Do this three times. Count 4. Swing arms outward and to the sides, shoulder height, palms up. Return to starting position. NOTE: This is a bouncy, rhythmic action, counting "one-and-two-and-three-and-*four*."

Time: Repeat five to ten times.

Benefits: Strengthens muscles of upper back and shoulders; stretches chest muscles; encourages good posture and prevents "dowager's hump."

Wall Push-Away

Starting Position: Stand erect with feet about six inches apart and arms straight, facing a wall; place palms on wall, and lean weight slightly forward.

Action: Count 1. Bend elbows and lower your body slowly toward the wall, while turning head to the side, until your cheek almost touches the wall. Count 2. Push against the wall with your arms and return to starting position. NOTE: Keep heels on floor throughout the exercise.

Time: Repeat ten times, then walk for five minutes.

Benefits: Increases strength of arm, shoulder and upper-back muscles; stretches muscles in chest and backs of legs.

Lying Leg Bend

Starting Position: Lie on back, legs extended with feet together; place arms at sides.

Action: Count 1. Bend left knee and move left foot in toward the buttocks, keeping the foot in light contact with the floor. Count 2. Lift knee toward chest as far as possible, using abdominal, hip and leg muscles; then clasp knee with both hands and pull slowly toward chest. Count 3. Return to position at end of Count 1. Count 4. Return to starting position. NOTE: After completing desired number of leg bends with one leg, repeat the exercise using the other leg.

Time: Repeat five to ten times, each leg.

Benefits: Improves flexibility of knee and hip joints; strengthens abdominal and hip muscles.

Leg Raise and Bend

Starting Position: Lie on back, legs extended and feet together; place arms at sides.

Action: Count 1. Raise extended left leg about

twelve inches off the floor. Count 2. Bend knee and move knee toward chest as far as possible, using abdominal, hip and leg muscles; then clasp knee with both hands and pull slowly toward chest. Count 3. Return to position at end of Count 1. Count 4. Return to starting position.

Time: Repeat two to five times.

Benefits: Improves flexibility of knee and hip joints; strengthens abdominal muscles.

Angel Stretch

Starting Position: Lie on back, legs straight with feet together; extend arms at sides.

Action: Count 1. Slide arms and legs outward along the floor to a spread-eagle position. Do not raise them. Count 2. Return to starting position. NOTE: Throughout the exercise try to press the lower back against the floor by tightening the abdominal muscles. Do not arch your lower back.

Time: Repeat five times.

Benefits: Stretches muscles of arms, legs and trunk; improves posture; builds up abdominal muscles.

Straight Line Walk

Starting Position: Stand erect and place left foot on a straight line; hold arms away from body to aid balance.

Action: Count 1. Walk the length of the line by putting your right foot in front of your left with your right heel touching your left toe; alternate your feet one in front of the other, heel-to-toe. Count 2. Return to the starting point by walking backward along the line, alternately placing one foot behind the other, toe-to-heel.

Time: Walk for ten feet.

Benefits: Improves balance; helps posture.

Walk the Beam

Starting Position: Stand erect with your left foot on a flat 2 x 6-inch board, the long axis of your foot parallel to the board.

Action: Count 1. Walk the length of the board by putting your right foot in front of your left with right heel touching your left toe; alternate your feet one in front of the other, heel-to-toe. Count 2. Return to starting point by walking backward along the length of the board, alternately placing one foot behind the other, toe-to-heel. NOTE: Place board flat on the floor, not on its edge.

Time: Five round-trip walks.

Benefits: Improves balance and posture.

Hop

Starting Position: Stand erect, weight on right foot, left leg bent slightly at the knee and left foot held a few inches off the floor; hold arms slightly away from the sides of the body to aid balance.

Action: Count 1. Hop several times on right foot, moving a few inches forward on each hop. Count 2. Change to left foot and hop, moving a few inches forward on each hop.

Time: Hop five times on each foot.

Benefits: Improves balance; strengthens extensor muscles of leg and foot; increases circulation.

Knee Push-Up

Starting Position: Lie on floor, face down, legs together, knees bent with feet raised off floor; place hands on floor under shoulders, palms down.

Action: Count 1. Push upper body off floor until arms are fully extended and body is a straight line from head to knees. Count 2. Return to starting position.

Time: Repeat three to six times.

Benefits: Strengthens muscles of arms, shoulders and trunk.

Side Leg Raise

Starting Position: Lie with right side of body on floor, head resting on right arm.

Action: Lift leg about thirty inches off the floor. Count 2. Return to starting position. NOTE: Repeat the desired number of times and then turn over on left side and exercise your right leg.

Time: Repeat five to ten times with each leg.

Benefits: Improves flexibility of the hip joint, strengthens lateral muscles of trunk and hip.

Head and Shoulder Curl

Starting Position: Lie on back, legs straight, feet together; extend arms along the front of the legs with palms resting lightly on your thighs.

Action: Count 1. Tighten abdominal muscles and lift head and shoulders so that shoulders are about ten inches off the floor. Meanwhile, slide arms along down your legs, keeping them extended. Hold the position for four seconds. Count 2. Return slowly to starting position, keeping abdominal muscles tight until shoulders and head rest on floor. Relax.

Time: Repeat two to five times; hold for four seconds.

Benefits: Relieves congestion of joints; loosens back muscles.

Diver's Stance

Starting Position: Stand erect, feet slightly apart; place arms at sides.

Action: Count 1. Rise on toes and bring arms upward and forward so that they are parallel to the floor, palms down. Count 2. Close eyes and balance in this position for ten seconds. NOTE: Hold your head straight and keep your body firm throughout the exercise.

Time: Hold position for ten seconds.

Benefits: Improves balance; strengthens extensor muscles of feet and legs; maintains good posture.

Stork Stand

Starting Position: Stand erect, feet slightly apart; place hands on hips, hold head straight.

Action: Count 1. Transfer weight to the left foot and bend right knee, bringing the sole of the right foot to the inner side of the left knee. Count 2. Close eyes and hold this position for ten seconds. NOTE: Change to the right leg and repeat.

Time: Hold position ten seconds on each leg.

Benefits: Improves overall body balance.

Alternate Walk-Jog

Starting Position: Assume ordinary walking position.

Action: Walk fifty steps, jog ten steps.

Time: From one to three minutes.

Benefits: Provides an interval of exercise for the circulatory system; strengthens leg muscles.

Swimming and Water Exercises

Swimming is such a good activity, it deserves special mention. All the major muscle groups are involved; exercise can be adjusted from very mild to strenuous.

Work out your own system of interval training, with your doctor's guidance. For example, swim across a pool, get out, walk around to the other side and swim back. Repeat these trips until your swimming totals a good distance.

Next, try swimming the length of the pool. Walk back and swim another length. You can use different strokes for each lap. Your buoyancy in the water will make it easier to do some exercises.

Other Exercises to Try

To improve foot and leg health, here are some more-strenuous activities. Be sure to get your doctor's approval for these exercises:

"Bicycling": Lie on the floor and use your arms and elbows to support your hips. Pedal your feet in the air. Do not try this if you think you will have difficulty supporting your weight.

Riding a bicycle (choose a safe area).

Pedaling a stationary bike.

Playing golf. (A golf cart can be used.)

Exercising on wall pulley-weights or a rowing machine.

Passing a medicine ball with a partner while standing or seated, or bouncing the ball off a wall in continuous rhythmic movement.

CHAPTER 10

HYDROTHERAPY AT HOME

Water in combination with warmth has a therapeutic effect on arthritic conditions. This guideline is offered by Walter S. McClellan, M.D., in *Cyclopedia of Medicine*.

"The treatment of a patient with arthritis with physical medicine including heat, massage and exercise stands out as one of the most universally valuable forms of therapy. Hydrotherapy (baths) offers a valuable adjunct both for the provision of heat and a medium for exercise."

When you immerse yourself in comfortably warm water or use hot and cold applications, according to Dr. McClellan, pain is reduced and health restored. Hydrotherapy results in increased elimination of waste products through the skin and kidneys; improved circulation of the blood and other body fluids (heat expands the blood vessels), and a mechanical breaking-down of adhesions and softening of any thickening in muscles and tissues.

Remember that any exercise, hydrotherapy and activity is important to keep muscles working. Inactive muscles lose their function; this reduces activity and pain increases as mobility is reduced. Activity is a protection against stiffness.

Since arthritics complain most frequently of stiff joints, a comfortably hot bath can be helpful. This form of moist heat will initiate the loosening of constricted joints, enabling freer motion.

Aim for a happy medium. Water should be neither too hot nor too cold. To avoid abusing your already aching body here are some suggestions for home hydrotherapy:

Apply a cold compress or an ice bag (put ice cubes in a plastic bag wrapped in a towel) and apply to the painful area. Relief comes when the pain is numbed.

Apply heat with an infrared lamp, heating pad, hot compress or tub bath to the painful area. Continue until you feel relief. Heat relaxes the muscles, thus soothing the spasm.

Daily, enjoy the simple luxury of a warm tub bath. This supplies uniform heat to widely separated joints at the same time. Do not use too-hot water. Do not remain in the tub longer than twenty or thirty minutes since this can be tiring.

Apply local heat by soaking a piece of wool or a towel in hot water. Wring out thoroughly and cover the painful joint. To retain heat longer, wrap plastic sheeting over the compress.

To heal a single part of your body, try a 250-watt infrared reflector heat bulb. (Do not use an ultraviolet or sun lamp.) Place it about three feet from the skin surface. Let the warmth penetrate. Use no longer than thirty minutes at a time.

Heating pads are helpful if they are in good condition. Use *low* or *medium* heat (unless otherwise advised by your physician) and only for short periods of time. Do not lie down on a heating pad since this may be too warm. Do not go to sleep with a heating pad on any part of your body.

BATHS FOR ARTHRITIC RELIEF

There are various home baths and heat treatments beneficial to arthritics. Only one requires special ingredients; two are devices that can be installed in the home.

Paraffin Baths

The Arthritis Foundation offers these guidelines: "Paraffin baths are particularly useful for stiff or inflamed hands or wrists. But do not use paraffin if you have any open cuts or wounds on your hands."

To prepare a paraffin bath (as per instructions offered by the foundation), put four pounds of paraffin wax and two ounces of mineral oil into the upper part of a three-quart double boiler (with plenty of water in the bottom section). Heat until the wax is melted. Remove from the heat and allow the wax to cool until a thin white coating appears on top. It is then ready for use.

When heating paraffin, be extremely careful to keep it away from an open flame. Never melt it in a pot directly over the flame; always use a double boiler.

With your fingers slightly separated, dip your hands, one at a time, quickly into and out of the paraffin. Re-dip them seven or eight times, allowing the wax to cool on your hands between dippings. Once you have started to dip, do not move your fingers because this will cause the paraffin to crack.

Have someone wrap your hands in a plastic bag or paper towel and hold them still for about twenty minutes. The wax will crack and peel off cleanly and can be returned to the boiler for reuse. Paraffin may be applied to larger joints with a paint brush.

Feel-Good Baths

Morning aches are a sign that metabolism is still sluggish. A good bath will get the circulation going in every weary muscle. Comfortably warm water brings the blood to the skin quickly. Scrubbing with a soapy brush speeds circulation as does a brisk toweling afterwards.

Weariness and pain at the end of the day can be relieved with a warm bath. Take ten minutes out, soaping yourself well to remove toxic wastes that have accumulated throughout the day. These few minutes stretched out in the tub will wash away many of the aches that make you feel tired.

Here's a bath that has no schedule. Whenever nervous fatigue causes arthritic flareup, or unaccustomed activity makes muscles stiff and sore or bad weather leaves you wet and chilled, you can get rid of these aches with a long, comfortably hot soak in the tub. Use bath salts and soak leisurely. Drink a glass of water before getting into the tub; this encourages perspiration and washing out of toxic wastes. You will feel your muscles unkink. Replenish the hot water by letting the faucet run once or twice.

If you're so uncomfortable that sleep is an impossibility, try a "lullaby" soak. First have a light snack of raw fruits or vegetables. The digestive process will draw the blood to internal organs and away from the brain. Do everything slowly. Get into a tub of mildly warm water. Use a washcloth in slow motion. Avoid the brush since it may be too stimulating. Lie back and let your muscles be soothed by the scented water. Blot yourself dry gently and slip into bed.

Soak a towel in a basin of hot water and rub your body well. Wring out the towel in cold water and wipe yourself thoroughly. Using a towel in this way will revive your sluggish metabolism and make you fell better all over.

Treat your aching feet to a warm soak and a vigorous scrubbing. This acts as an all-over tonic increasing circulation and soothing pains. Soaking and scrubbing will relax your feet — and the rest of your body as well.

Whirlpool Bath

Whirlpool units similar to those used in health clubs and spas can be installed in your own bathtub but be sure to get permission from your doctor. The bath massages all of your muscles with no effort on your part. You just sit there and let the whirlpool exercise your body. It revives a sluggish metabolism and is soothing for aches and arthritic pains.

Sauna Bath

A stall-shower-sized unit can be put right in your home. Again, be sure your doctor approves. Saunas offer dry heat therapy, with temperatures going as high as 200°F. This might not be too helpful for your particular condition but it is worth checking it out with a physician.

HOME HYDROTHERAPY

Mildred McKie, M.D., in *Natural Aids For Common Ills*, recommends the use of hydrotherapy to ease arthritic pain. Dr. McKie offers these suggestions for home use:

Soaking. Immerse your hands or feet in comfortably warm water for ten minutes, three times daily (or more often) to reduce pain, muscle fatigue and strain. Keep pushing the water with your hands to create a soothing current.

Wet Compress. Soak a cloth in water, squeeze, then apply to the aching part. Change every five minutes. Use either comfortably hot or cold water or alternate for a stimulating reaction.

Sitz Bath. Either the first thing in the morning or the last thing at night, sit in three inches of warm water for three minutes while dangling legs over the edge of the tub. Keep legs and body warm and dry. This will help redistribute sluggish blood and improve metabolism.

Wet Pack. "Short, frequent packs are stimulating; longer packs are sedative," says Dr. McKie. "In subnormal body temperature . . . packs are indicated to relieve inner congestion and pain (and) to induce sleep or promote elimination."

To make a wet pack, first cover the bed with a plastic sheet. Boil water in a large kettle to remove impurities such as chlorine. As the water cools, fold a few thicknesses of blanket lengthwise so you can roll them over quickly when you lie down.

After removing your clothes, take two single white sheets, dip them in the hot water and wring out. Wrap one around your back and the other across the front of your body.

Lie down while the sheets are warm. Wrap yourself like a mummy. One arm should remain out only long enough so that you can cover yourself with the blankets.

At first, you'll feel the coldness of the wet sheets. But slowly, they will warm and you will feel drowsy and relaxed. You may even doze off. NOTE: Set the alarm so that you have only *one hour* of this wet-pack treatment. Dr. McKie feels that the drawn-out toxins from the body may be reabsorbed if you remain longer than one hour.

When you get up, rub yourself briskly with a bath towel. Run a tub with warm water and treat yourself to a five-minute scrub to get rid of any accumulated wastes. Then, get into bed (with plastic sheets removed, of course) and have a good night's sleep. The next morning, you can wash the wet sheets in boiling hot water to sterilize them.

Dr. McKie says that when an arthritic uses this wet pack home healer, it will cleanse the skin of toxic wastes excreted by perspiration, improve elimination, circulation and general metabolism, and induce heat radiations through the skin to regulate the body's temperature.

Regular wet-pack treatments should help wash away impurities and more important, strike at the cause of arthritic pain — incorrect metabolism.

CHAPTER 11.

HEALTHY COOKING FOR ARTHRITICS

TO COMBAT ARTHRITIS, the entire body must be made well. Healthy food is the key to correcting any errors in metabolism and setting off the chain reaction that helps the body's clocks adjust. The goal is an overall rhythm in all functions.

In the following recipes, the emphasis is on one word: *natural*. Foods purchased, prepared and served should be as close to their original state as possible. Ingredients used in recipes should be pure and unrefined. By introducing healthy food to your body, you will give it a source of nutrition that will ward off arthritis as well as other ailments.

Healthy foods give your body the necessary materials for building and repair, for regulation of vital processes and for the creation of needed warmth and energy. You will also discover a new world of delicious taste and remarkable freshness when you feast on natural foods.

The recipes included in this section emphasize whole, natural foods. It's easy to make these simple adjustments. Use whole grains instead of refined flours and cereals. Honey and any natural sweetener such as molasses or fruit puree can replace refined white sugar. Herbs and spices substitute for salt and pepper. Use cold-pressed plant or vegetable oils rather than hard animal fats, and yeast instead of baking powder and baking soda.

Raise the nutritional value and enhance the taste of almost any recipe by adding seeds, chopped nuts, sprouts, wheat germ, bran, brewer's yeast, kelp or unflavored gelatin powder.

A few of the items are available in the health-food sections of larger supermarkets. You can also purchase these foods in any local health-food store. There are a number of unrefined foods made without additives, preservatives or chemicals on the shelves of health stores. If packaged, the label will attest to their purity. Otherwise, check that food is as fresh and free of processing as possible.

Change your approach to food preparation. Instead of buying commercial applesauce which is usually laden with sugar, buy a bag of fresh apples. At home, wash, core and slice the apples and boil them in water until they are soft. Add honey to taste. Or, simply blend the washed sliced apples. In a few moments, you'll have a natural applesauce which has no taste rival.

AVOCADO DIP

2 tablespoons onion, diced
2 tablespoons water
2 ripe avocados, peeled and pitted
1/4 cup tomato, diced
1/4 cup health store mayonnaise
3 tablespoons lemon juice
1 1/4 teaspoons sea salt
1 clove garlic, crushed

Mix onion with water. In a small mixing bowl, mash avocado. Add onion along with remaining ingredients; mix well. Serve with whole grain crackers, vegetables sticks, etc. Yield: About 2 cups.

MARINATED VEGETABLE ANTIPASTO

1 can (14 oz.) artichoke hearts, drained and halved
1 cup mushrooms, sliced
1 cup carrots, sliced and steamed
1 1/2 ounces olives, pitted
2 tablespoons pimiento, chopped
2/3 cup apple cider vinegar
2/3 cup olive or vegetable oil
2 tablespoons onion, chopped

1 teaspoon sea salt   ¹/4 clove garlic, crushed
1 teaspoon honey

In a small bowl, combine artichokes, mushrooms, carrots, olives, pimiento; set aside. In a small saucepan combine remaining ingredients. Bring to a boil. Cool slightly. Pour over vegtables. Cover and refrigerate at least 12 hours or longer. Yield: About 1 quart.

PAPRIKA CHEESE STICKS

1¹/2 cups all-purpose un-   ¹/2 cup (4 ounces) mild ched-
   bleached flour, sifted   dar cheese, grated
1 tablespoon paprika   ¹/2 cup vegetable oil
¹/2 teaspoon sea salt   3 tablespoons cold water

Preheat oven to very hot (450° F.). In a mixing bowl, sift together flour, paprika, and sea salt. Blend in cheese. Add oil and mix until combined. Sprinkle in water, 1 teaspoon at a time, mixing lightly after each addition. (Add only enough water to hold together.) Shape into a ball, being careful not to handle too much. Roll out dough ¹/4-inch thick on a lightly floured board. Cut into 3 x ¹/2-inch strips. Place on ungreased cookie sheet. Bake 8 to 10 minutes. Cool on racks. Yield: About 4¹/2 dozen sticks.

LIPTAUER CHEESE
(Austrian Spread)

1 tablespoon onion diced   1 teaspoon capers, finely
1 tablespoon water   minced
2 teaspoons warm water   1 tablespoon caraway seed
¹/2 cup vegetable oil   1 tablespoon parsley,
1 cup yogurt   chopped
2 anchovy fillets, finely   ¹/2 teaspoon paprika
   minced

Soak onion in tablespoon of water for 10 minutes. Add warm water. Pour oil into a small mixing bowl and add yogurt, blending well. Now add onion and remaining ingredients except parsley and paprika;

mix thoroughly. Pack into a 2-cup bowl or mold; chill until firm. To unmold, dip quickly in hot water. Turn out onto a serving dish. Garnish with parsley and paprika. Serve with whole grain bread slices or whole grain crackers. Yield: About 2 cups cheese spread.

SPICED GARBANZOS
(Chick Peas)

1 tablespoon onion, diced
1 tablespoon water
1 1/2 cups chick peas, cooked
1 clove garlic, crushed

Soak diced onion in water for 10 minutes. In a small bowl, combine onion with remaining ingredients; toss gently. Chill and serve. Yield: 2 cups.

GAZPACHO

1 cup water or vegetable broth
3 medium tomatoes (1 pound), peeled and diced
1 cucumber, peeled and sliced
1 small green pepper, seeded and diced
1 small onion, chopped
2 cloves garlic, crushed
1/4 cup olive oil
2 tablespoons apple cider vinegar

In jar of electric blender combine water, tomatoes, cucumber, pepper, onion and garlic; blend until amost smooth. Stir in oil and vinegar. Chill well. Serve in bowls garnished with whole grain bread chunks, diced tomato and cucumber and chopped parsley, if desired. Serves 4.

NEW ENGLAND FISH CHOWDER

1/4 cup onion, diced
3 1/2 cups water
2 tablespoons oil
2 cups potatoes, sliced
2 teaspoons sea salt
1 clove garlic, crushed
2 cups milk
2 tablespoons unbleached flour
2 small bay leaves
2 pounds fish fillets, cut into chunks
2 tablespoons parsley, chopped
1/2 teaspoon paprika

Combine onion with one-half cup water for 10 minutes. In a large saucepan, heat oil. Add onion-water mixture and sauté 5 minutes. Remove from heat; add remaining 3 cups water, potatoes, sea salt and garlic. Bring to a boil. Reduce heat; cover and simmer 15 minutes or until potatoes are almost tender. Combine milk and flour. Slowly stir into saucepan; add bay leaves and fish. Simmer, do not boil, 15 minutes or until fish flakes are fork-tested. Remove bay leaves. Sprinkle with parsley and paprika. Serves 6 to 8.

GERMAN CABBAGE SOUP

2 cups homemade beef broth	1/3 cup onion, diced
1 cup tomato juice	1 tablespoon caraway seed
2 teaspoons lemon juice	1 teaspoon honey
3 cups cabbage, shredded	1 clove garlic, crushed
2 cups apples, diced	

In large saucepan combine broth, tomato juice and lemon juice; bring to a boil. Add remaining ingredients. Cover and simmer 20 minutes. Serve with sliced whole rye bread, if desired. Serves 6.

BLACK BEAN SOUP

1 cup dried black beans	1 teaspoon garlic, crushed
10 cups water	1 teaspoon oregano leaves
1/4 pound fat-free beef slices	1/2 teaspoon cumin seed
3/4 teaspoon warm water	2 tablespoons lemon juice
1/3 cup onion, diced	1 teaspoon sea salt
1/2 red pepper, seeded and diced	4 tablespoons parsley, chopped

In a Dutch oven or large heavy saucepan combine beans, water and beef. Bring to a boil. Reduce heat, cover and simmer 2 1/2 hours or until beans are just tender. Now add warm water to cooked beans along with onion, pepper, garlic, oregano and cumin. Cover and simmer 30 minutes or until beans are very tender. If soup is too thick, add more water. Stir in lemon juice and sea salt. Sprinkle with parsley. If desired, garnish with chopped hard-cooked egg. Serves 6.

HEARTY BEEF AND VEGETABLE SOUP

3 pounds soup meat with
    bone
1 1/2 pounds soup bones (good
    calcium source)
1/4 cup celery, chopped
4 tablespoons parsley,
    chopped

1 large bay leaf
1 1/2 cups tomatoes, sliced
1/3 cup onion, diced
3 cups cabbage, diced
2 cups carrots, sliced
3 medium potatoes, peeled
    and diced

In a large saucepan combine soup meat, bones and water to cover (about 10 cups). Bring to a boil; skim off foam. Tie celery, parsley and bay leaf in a cheesecloth bag; add to soup along with tomatoes and onion. Cover and simmer 2 to 2 1/2 hours or until meat is tender. Add remaining vegetables and cook 30 to 40 minutes longer or until vegetables are tender. Remove and discard herb bag. Remove meat and bones. Cut meat into chunks and return to saucepan along with bones still containing marrow, if desired. Serves 6 to 8.

CAESAR SALAD

3 tablespoons vegetable oil
1 clove garlic, crushed
2 cups bran
1 head (1 1/4 pounds)
    Romaine lettuce
3 tablespoons olive or salad
    oil

2 tablespoons lemon juice
1 egg
1/2 cup Parmesan cheese,
    grated
3 anchovy fillets, diced

In a small skillet heat oil; stir in garlic. Add bran and sauté briefly; set aside. Tear lettuce into bite-size pieces (makes 3 quarts). Place in large salad bowl. Combine oil and lemon juice; mix well. Pour over lettuce. Break egg into center of salad. Toss well. Add bran mixture, cheese and anchovies. Toss gently; serve immediately. Serves 8.

FRENCH SALAD DRESSING

3/4 cup vegetable or olive oil
1 1/2 teaspoons paprika
1 1/2 teaspoons chives, minced
1 1/2 teaspoons basil leaves, crumbled

2 cloves garlic, crushed
3 tablespoons apple cider vinegar
2 tablespoons lemon juice

Combine oil, paprika, chives, basil and garlic. Gradually stir in vinegar and lemon juice. Mix thoroughly before pouring over salad. Yield: 1 cup.

LOW-CALORIE TOMATO SALAD DRESSING

3/4 cup tomato juice, chilled
2 tablespoons lemon juice
2 tablespoons onion, diced
1 tablespoon basil leaves, crumbled

1/2 teaspoon sea salt
1 clove garlic, crushed
1/8 teaspoon ground cumin seed

In a small jar combine all ingredients; blend well. Pour over mixed salad greens; toss well. Yield: 1 cup.

POTATO SALAD, HUNGARIAN STYLE

3 tablespoons onion, chopped
3 tablespoons water
4 cups potatoes, peeled, diced and cooked
1/2 cup cucumber, peeled and diced
1/4 cup radishes, diced

4 hard-cooked eggs
3/4 cup yogurt
1 tablespoon cider vinegar
3 teaspoons paprika
1 1/4 teaspoons sea salt
1 teaspoon celery seed
1 teaspoon poppy seed

Soak onion in water for 10 minutes. In a large salad bowl combine potatoes, cucumber and radishes; set aside. Separate egg yolks from whites. Dice egg whites and add to vegetable mixture along with onion. In a small bowl mash yolks. Stir in yogurt, vinegar, 2 teaspoons of the paprika, sea salt, celery, poppy seeds; mix well. Add to vegetables; toss gently. Chill thoroughly. Sprinkle with remaining teaspoon of paprika before serving. Serves 6 or 8.

FRUIT-FLAVORED CHICKEN SALAD

3 tablespoons onion, diced
3 tablespoons water
2 tablespoons vegetable oil
1 teaspoon curry powder
1/3 cup health store mayonnaise
1 tablespoon lemon juice
1/2 teaspoon sea salt

3 cups cooked chicken (or turkey), chilled and diced
1 cup pineapple chunks
1/2 cup nuts, coarsely chopped
1/3 cup seedless, sun-dried raisins
1 apple, cored and diced

Soak onion in water for 10 minutes. In a small skillet, heat oil. Add onion and curry. Sauté 3 to 5 minutes: cool. Combine curry mixture with mayonnaise, lemon juice, sea salt; mix well; set aside. In a large salad bowl combine chicken, pineapple, nuts, raisins and apple. Add curried dressing and toss gently. Serve in lettuce-lined salad bowl and garnish with shredded coconut, if desired. Serves 6.

CREAMY CELERY SEED DRESSING

1/2 cup yogurt
2 tablespoons milk
1 teaspoon chives
3/4 teaspoon celery seed

1/4 teaspoon sea salt
1 tablespoon apple cider vinegar

In a small bowl combine yogurt, milk, chives, celery seed and salt substitute. Mix well. Blend in vinegar. Serve with vegetable salads, cucumbers, tomatoes, tossed mixed greens, etc. Yield: About 1/2 cup.

BELGIAN SMOTHERED POTATOES

6 large potatoes
1/2 cup vegetable oil
3 tablespoons grape juice

1 teaspoon onion powder
3/4 teaspoon sea salt
1 tablespoon chives; minced

Peel and quarter potatoes. In a heavy skillet, heat oil. Add potatoes and remaining ingredients except chives. Cover tightly. Cook over low heat for 45 minutes; remove cover; add chives. If any cooking liquid remains, turn heat high so that moisture evaporates. Serves 6.

RATATOUILLE PROVENCALE
(Baked Mixed Vegetables)

1/2 cup onion, diced	*3/4 cup olive or vegetable oil*
1/2 teaspoon garlic, minced	*1 cup tomato wedges*
1/3 cup water	*4 tablespoons parsley,*
1 medium (1 pound) eggplant	*chopped*
1 pound zucchini	*1 teaspoon oregano leaves*

Soak onion and garlic in water for 10 minutes. Remove stem end of eggplant and cut into 1/2-inch cubes. Cut zucchini into 1/2 inch slices. In a large skillet or heavy saucepan heat oil. Stir in onion and garlic; sauté 2 minutes. Add eggplant and zucchini; sauté 8 minutes, stirring frequently, adding more oil if needed. Blend in tomatoes, parsley, and oregano. Cover and simmer 45 to 60 minutes. When vegetables are soft remove to serving dish; use liquid as a natural sauce or topping. Serve hot or cold. Serves 6.

LOW-CALORIE CREOLE CABBAGE

1 medium head (2 pounds)	*3/4 teaspoon oregano leaves,*
cabbage	*crumbled*
1 cup tomato wedges	*2 teaspoons lemon juice*
2 tablespoons onion, diced	

Shred cabbage (makes 2 quarts). Place 1/2-inch boiling water in a medium saucepan. Add cabbage; cover and cook 10 minutes; drain. Meanwhile, in another saucepan combine tomatoes, onion and oregano. Bring to a boil. Reduce heat and simmer, uncovered, 15 minutes. Stir in lemon juice. Add tomato mixture to cabbage; toss gently. Serve hot. Serves 8.

SKEWERED VEGETABLE MEDLEY

1/2 cup olive or vegetable oil　　*1/2 small eggplant, cut into*
1/4 cup apple juice　　　　　　　　*1-inch cubes*
2 tablespoons water　　　　　*1 medium zucchini, sliced*
2 tablespoons onion, minced　　*1/2-inch thick*
1/4 teaspoon garlic, minced　　*12 cherry tomatoes*
1/2 pound mushrooms

Preheat broiler. In a small bowl combine oil, apple juice, water, onion and garlic; let stand for 10 minutes. Arrange mushrooms, eggplant and zucchini alternately on skewers; brush vegetables generously with seasoned oil mixture. Cook under hot broiler 10 to 15 minutes, turning and brushing occasionally. Five minutes before vegetables are tender, place 2 cherry tomatoes at the end of each skewer. Serves 6.

GINGER-GLAZED CARROTS

6 large carrots　　　　　　*1/4 cup butter*
1 cup water　　　　　　　　*1/4 cup honey*
1 teaspoon ground ginger

Peel carrots; cut into strips 2-inches long by 1/4-inch-wide. In a medium saucepan combine water and half of the ginger. Bring to boiling point. Add carrots, lower heat and steam 8 to 10 minutes or until carrots are almost tender. Drain if necessary. In a medium skillet melt butter. Stir in honey and remaining ginger. Add carrots and cook, stirring frequently, 8 minutes or until carrots are tender and glazed. Serves 6.

SMA KOTTBULLAR
(Swedish Meatballs)

1/4 cup onion, diced　　　　*1/2 pound ground lean veal*
1/4 cup water　　　　　　　*1/2 pound ground lean lamb*
4 tablespoons vegetable oil　*1/2 teaspoon dill seed or*
1 cup bran or wheat germ　　*1 tablespoon chopped*
2 cups light cream　　　　　*dill*
1 pound ground lean beef

*2 tablespoons chopped
    parsley*
1 egg, beaten

*1 tablespoon unbleached
    flour*

Soak onion in water for 10 minutes. In a large skillet heat half the oil. Add onion and sauté for 5 minutes. Soak bran in 1 cup of the cream. In a large mixing bowl combine sautéed onion, bran mixture, meats, herbs and egg. Do not overmix. Shape mixture into 1½-inch balls. In the same skillet, heat remaining oil. Add meatballs and brown well, turning gently to retain shape and adding more oil if needed. Remove meatballs to a serving dish; keep warm. Stir flour into skillet; brown lightly. Gradually add the remaining 1 cup cream, stirring constantly. Strain, if desired. Pour over meatballs and serve. Yield: About 36 meatballs.

CHICKEN CACCIATORE

2 tablespoons olive oil
*2 (2½ to 3-pound each)
    chickens,   cut   into
    eighths*
½ cup onion, diced
1 teaspoon garlic, minced
⅓ cup water

1 cup tomato wedges
1 cup tomato juice
*1½ teaspoons oregano
    leaves, crumbled*
3 small bay leaves
½ cup fruit juice

In a Dutch oven or large heavy skillet heat oil. Add chicken, a few pieces at a time and brown well on all sides. Meanwhile, soak onion and garlic in water for 10 minutes. Add onion and garlic to Dutch oven and sauté for 5 minutes. Return all of the chicken to the Dutch oven. Add tomatoes, tomato juice, oregano and bay leaves; mix gently. Cover and simmer 45 minutes or until chicken is tender. Remove chicken to serving platter. Cover with foil to keep warm. Add fruit juice to sauce in Dutch oven. Simmer uncovered 10 minutes. Remove bay leaves. Spoon sauce over chicken. Serve with steamed brown rice. Serves 6.

CHICKEN WITH RICE

1/2 cup onion, diced
1/4 cup green pepper, chopped
2/3 cup water
1/3 cup vegetable oil
1 (21/2 to 3-pound) chicken, cut into serving pieces
1 cup tomato wedges
1/2 cup soybeans (or other beans), cooked

1/4 cup olives, sliced
1 teaspoon oregano leaves
1/2 teaspoon paprika
1 clove garlic, crushed
3 cups boiling water
1 cup raw brown rice
1 cup shelled green peas

Soak onion and pepper in water for 10 minutes. Meanwhile, in a large saucepan heat oil. Add chicken and brown on all sides. Add onion; sauté about 5 minutes. Add tomatoes, beans, olives and seasonings and stir gently. Cover and simmer 10 minutes. Add boiling water and rice. Stir. Cover and continue simmering until chicken is almost tender, 20 to 25 minutes. Mix in peas. Cook 10 minutes longer. Place in serving casserole. Serves 6.

CREOLE JAMBALAYA

1 (21/3 to 3-pound) chicken, cut into serving pieces.
4 cups water
1/3 cup onion, diced
1/4 teaspoon garlic, minced
1/2 pound vegetarian-style meatless frankfurters (available in health-food stores)

1 tablespoon unbleached flour
1 cup tomato wedges
4 tablespoons parsley, chopped
1 small bay leaf
1/2 teaspoon thyme leaves
11/4 cups raw, brown rice
1/2 pound beef, cooked and julienned

In a saucepan simmer chicken in 3 cups of the water until almost tender, about 35 to 40 minutes. Remove chicken from broth; reserve 21/2 cups of the broth and the chicken. Soak onion and garlic in remaining water for 10 minutes; set aside. Cut meatless frankfurters into 1/2-inch pieces. In a large Dutch oven or heavy saucepan, brown frankfurters; remove and set aside. Pour off most of fat. Add onion and garlic; sauté 5 minutes. Stir in flour. Gradually add reserved broth. Add tomatoes, parsley, bay leaf and thyme. Bring to a boil. Add reserved chicken and frankfurters along with the rice and beef; stir gently. Reduce heat. Cover and simmer 20 minutes or until rice and chicken are tender. Serves 8.

CHICKEN CURRY

1/2 cup onion, diced
1/3 cup water
4 tablespoons vegetable oil
4 tablespoons ground coriander
1 3/4 teaspoons ground cumin seed
1 3/4 teaspoons ground turmeric

1 teaspoon ground cardamon seed
1/2 teaspoon ground ginger
4 pounds chicken legs or breasts
1 1/2 cups hot chicken broth or bouillon
1/3 cup evaporated or coconut milk
2 teaspoons lemon juice

Soak onion in water for 10 minutes. In a large skillet or Dutch oven, heat oil. Add onion and sauté until golden. Blend spices together. Add to onion and sauté 1/2 minute. Add chicken; cook, turning occasionally, for 5 minutes. Blend in broth. Cover and simmer 45 minutes or until chicken is tender. Remove chicken to a warm platter. Reduce liquid by half. Just before serving add milk. Cook only until hot. Add lemon juice. Pour sauce over chicken. Serve with brown rice, if desired. Serves 6 to 8.

PICADINHO
(Brazilian Ground Beef)

1/4 cup onion, diced
1/4 cup water
1 tablespoon olive or vegetable oil
1 1/2 pounds ground lean beef
2 cups tomatoes, chopped

3/4 teaspoon oregano leaves
1/4 to 1/2 cup beef broth
1 medium-size boiled potato, peeled and diced
1/4 cup olives, sliced
2 hard-cooked eggs, sliced

Soak onion in water for 10 minutes. In a large skillet, heat oil. Add onion and beef; saute until meat is brown. Add tomatoes and oregano. Stir in 1/4 cup of the broth; cover and simmer 30 minutes; add additional broth if mixture seems dry. Just before serving stir in potato and olives. Garnish with eggs. Serve with black beans or soybeans, or brown rice. Serves 6.

HUNGARIAN GOULASH

1/2 cup onion, diced
2 1/2 pounds lean boneless
beef stew meat
3 tablespoons vegetable oil
2 tablespoons paprika
1/4 teaspoon ground
marjoram

2 1/2 cups beef broth or water
3/4 cup grape juice
1/4 cup green pepper strips
1/4 cup unbleached flour

In a large Dutch oven or heavy skillet, combine onion with 2 tablespoons of the oil and saute 5 minutes. Remove onion; set aside. Add remaining oil to Dutch oven. Add meat, cut into 1 1/2-inch cubes, and brown well on all sides. Sprinkle with paprika and marjoram. Stir in broth, grape juice, pepper and reserved sauteed onion. Bring to a boil. Reduce heat; cover and simmer 2 hours or until meat is tender. Remove meat to serving platter. Strain gravy; mix flour with remaining 1/3 cup water. Gradually blend into gravy. Cook until thickened, stirring. Spoon over beef cubes. Serves 6.

LAMB KORMA

2 pounds boneless lamb stew
meat
1/2 cup plain yogurt
1 teaspoon ground cumin
seed
1 teaspoon ground turmeric
2/3 cup onion, diced

1/2 teaspoon garlic, minced
1 1/2 cups water
3 tablespoons vegetable oil
1 teaspoon curry powder
1 teaspoon lemon juice
2 tablespoons coconut,
shredded

Trim and discard excess fat from lamb; cut into 1-inch cubes. In a medium bowl combine yogurt, cumin and turmeric. Add lamb cubes. Cover and refrigerate one hour. Meanwhile, soak onion and garlic in $1/2$ cup of the water for 10 minutes. In a large skillet, heat oil. Add onion, garlic and curry powder. Sauté 5 minutes. Add meat. Cover skillet lightly; simmer 20 minutes. Add remaining 1 cup water. Stir to form a smooth gravy. Cover and continue cooking 25 minutes, or until lamb is tender. Stir in lemon juice and coconut just before serving. If desired, serve with brown rice. Serves 6.

GREEK BEEF STEW
(Stifado)

$2^1/2$ pounds lean boneless beef stew meat	3 tablespoons apple cider vinegar
3 tablespoons olive or vegetable oil	1 stick (4-inch) cinnamon, broken in half or $3/4$ teaspoon ground cinnamon
$1/2$ cup onion, diced	
3 tablespoons unbleached flour	
4 tablespoons water	4 whole cloves
1 cup tomato juice	2 teaspoons sea salt

Cut meat into 2-inch pieces. In a Dutch oven or large heavy saucepan, heat oil. Add meat and brown well on all sides. Add onion to meat and cook 3 minutes. Stir in flour and 2 tablespoons of the water; cook 2 minutes longer. Pour in remaining water along with tomato juice, vinegar and seasonings. Bring to a boil. Cover and reduce heat; simmer $1^1/2$ to 2 hours or until meat is tender. Remove cinnamon stick and cloves before serving. Serves 6.

FRENCH BEEF STEW

$2^1/2$ pounds boneless lean beef stew meat	$1/2$ cup onion, diced
	2 small bay leaves, crumbled
2 glasses fruit juice (berry juice, preferably)	1 teaspoon garlic, minced
	$1/2$ teaspoon thyme leaves

1/2 teaspoon rosemary leaves,   *1/4 cup unbleached flour*
   crumbled   *1 1/2 cups water*
2 tablespoons oil

Preheat oven to 400°F. (hot). Cut meat into 2-inch cubes. Place beef in a snug-fitting bowl or double plastic bag. Combine fruit juice, onion, bay leaves, minced garlic, thyme and rosemary. Pour over meat. Cover or seal; refrigerate 3 to 6 hours. Remove meat, reserving marinade. Dry meat on paper toweling. In a Dutch oven or heavy saucepan, heat oil. Add meat and brown over high heat 10 minutes, turning frequently. Stir flour into meat. Cook until flour is brown, stirring. Place Dutch oven, uncovered, in oven for 20 minutes. Reduce heat to slow (325°F.). Add reserved marinade and water. Cover and bake 1 1/2 hours or until meat is tender. Serves 6.

STEAK AU POIVRE

1 tablespoon paprika   *1 teaspoon sea salt*
4 pounds boned sirloin steak, *1/2 cup berry juice*
   2 inches thick

Rub paprika into both sides of steak. Let stand at room temperature for 30 minutes. Lightly oil a large heavy skillet. Heat until hot. Sprinkle both sides of steak with sea salt; place in skillet. Cook 8 to 10 minutes on each side or until desired doneness. Remove meat to serving platter. Add berry juice; cook and stir one minute. Pour over steak. Slice and serve. Serves 6 to 8.

VEAL PAPRIKASH

2 tablespoons onion, chopped   *1/4 cup vegetable oil*
Water   *2 tablespoons paprika*
2 pounds boneless veal   *1 tablespoon soybean oil*
   shoulder   *1/2 cup skim milk*
5 tablespoons unbleached   *1 cup plain yogurt*
   flour

Soak onion in 2 tablespoons water for 10 minutes.

Cut veal into 1-inch cubes. Dredge meat with 4 tablespoons of the flour. In a large skillet heat oil. Add meat, onion and 1 tablespoon of paprika. Brown meat on all sides. Add $1/3$ cup water. Cover tightly and simmer for 45 minutes or until meat is tender, turning occasionally. Add more water if needed. To make sauce, combine heated soybean oil with 1 tablespoon paprika. Cook and stir until mixture bubbles. Remove from heat and gradually stir in milk. Return to heat and bring rapidly to boiling point, stirring constantly. Reduce heat; cook and stir 1 to 2 minutes longer or until thickened. Gradually blend in yogurt, beating vigorously. Pour sauce over cooked meat in skillet and heat thoroughly but do not boil. Serves 6.

LOW-CALORIE BEEF AND VEGETABLE RAGOUT

*2 1/2 pounds boneless lean
   beef stew meat*
2 cups water
*2 beef bouillon cubes
   (natural variety, from
   health-food store)*

1/4 cup onion, diced
1/4 teaspoon garlic, minced
1 teaspoon thyme leaves
*1/2 pound fresh mushrooms,
   halved*
1/2 pound zucchini, sliced

Cut meat into 2-inch pieces. Arrange beef cubes on a rack in a broiler pan. Brown on all sides under a preheated hot broiler, about 15 to 20 minutes. Transfer meat to a Dutch oven or large heavy saucepan. Add water, bouillon cubes, onion, minced garlic and thyme; mix well. Bring to a boil. Reduce heat, cover and simmer $1 1/2$ hours. Add mushrooms and zucchini; simmer 30 minutes longer or until meat is done and vegetables are tender. Serves 8.

CHILI CHICKEN FRICASSEE

*2 (2 1/2 to 3-pound) chickens,
   cut into serving pieces*
2 cups water
1 cup tomato puree
1/2 cup black olives, sliced

1/4 cup celery, diced
1/4 cup green pepper, sliced
3 tablespoons onion, diced
2 tablespoons chili powder
1 tablespoon paprika

1 teaspoon oregano leaves

In a saucepan combine chicken with water. Bring to a boil. Cover, reduce heat and simmer until tender, about 1 hour. Remove chicken from saucepan; skim fat from broth; reserve 2 cups broth. Return broth to saucepan along with remaining ingredients. Simmer 10 minutes, uncovered. Add chicken and simmer 5 minutes longer or until chicken is hot. Serves 8.

SAN JOAQUIN OVEN ROAST

4 pounds bone-in chuck roast or steak
2 teaspoons sea salt
3/4 teaspoon marjoram leaves, crumbled
1/4 cup onion, chopped
2 tablespoons unbleached flour

Preheat oven to 500°F. (very hot). Sprinkle both sides of roast with sea salt and marjoram. Place in a roasting pan in oven. Brown on both sides, turning once, about 30 to 40 minutes. Sprinkle onions over top of meat. Cover; reduce heat to moderate (350°F.) and cook one hour or until tender. Measure pan drippings for gravy. Add sufficient water to measure 2 cups. Blend in flour; cook and stir until thickened. Serve with meat. Serves 6.

LOW-CALORIE YOGURT-BAKED CHICKEN

1 (2 1/2 to 3-pound) chicken, cut into serving pieces
1 cup plain yogurt
1 tablespoon onion, diced
2 tablespoons parsley, chopped
1 teaspoon sage leaves
1/2 teaspoon tarragon leaves
1/4 teaspoon garlic, minced
1 tablespoon water

Preheat oven to 425°F. (hot). Place chicken on a rack in a shallow roasting pan. Bake in oven for 45 minutes. Meanwhile, combine yogurt, onion, parsley, sage, tarragon and garlic with water. Remove chicken and rack from roasting pan; pour off and discard pan drippings. Return chicken to roasting pan without rack. Pour yogurt mixture over chicken. Reduce oven heat to slow (325°F.) and bake 20 minutes or until chicken is tender. Serves 4.

PARSLEYED OVEN POT ROAST

5 pounds bottom round of
  beef
2 cups tomato wedges
3/4 cup berry juice
1/4 cup onion, diced
4 tablespoons parsley,
  chopped

1 bay leaf
1/2 teaspoon garlic, minced
6 medium carrots, peeled and
  sliced
1 1/2 pounds zucchini, sliced
2 cups cherry tomatoes

Preheat oven to 450°F. (hot). Place meat, fat side down, in a heavy oven-proof casserole or Dutch oven. Brown well on all sides in the oven about 50 to 60 minutes. Drain off fat. Combine tomatoes, berry juice, onion, parsley, bay leaf and garlic. Pour over meat. Cover; reduce heat to moderate (350°F.) and bake 2 1/2 to 3 hours or until meat and vegetables are tender, adding the carrots 40 minutes before cooking time is up, the zucchini 20 minutes before and the cherry tomatoes 10 minutes before. Slice and serve with the vegetables. Serves 8 to 10.

HERBED BROILED FISH

1 tablespoon vegetable oil
2 tablespoons parsley,
  chopped
1/2 teaspoon oregano leaves,
  crumbled

1 tablespoon lemon juice
1 1/2 pounds fish steaks

Preheat broiler. In a small saucepan, heat oil. Add parsley flakes, oregano and lemon juice. Brush over both sides of fish. Arrange on a rack in a broiler pan. Place under hot broiler. Broil 10 minutes or until fish flakes easily when tested with a fork. Serves 4.

BROWN RICE PUDDING

1 quart milk
1/3 cup raw brown rice
2 eggs
2 egg yolks
1/2 cup honey

1 1/2 teaspoons pure vanilla extract
1/2 teaspoon ground cinnamon
1/4 teaspoon ground nutmeg

In a medium saucepan combine milk and rice. Bring just to boiling point. Cover, reduce heat and simmer 35 to 40 minutes or until rice is very tender. In a small mixing bowl beat eggs and egg yolks. Gradually beat in honey. Remove rice mixture from heat and slowly stir in egg mixture, being careful not to curdle it. Cook over low heat, stirring constantly, for 5 minutes or until mixture just begins to thicken and coats a metal spoon. Remove from heat; cool. Stir in vanilla extract, cinnamon and nutmeg. Chill. Serves 6 to 8.

Dietary Notes

_____

_____

_____

_____

_____

_____

_____

_____

_____

_____

_____

_____

_____

_____

_____

_____

_____

_____

_____

_____

_____

_____

_____

_____

_____

_____

_____

_____

_____

_____

_____

_____

_____

_____

_____

_____

_____

Dietary Notes

_____

_____

_____

_____

_____

_____

_____

_____

_____

_____

_____

_____

_____

_____

_____

_____

_____

_____

_____

Dietary Notes

HEALTH POWER IS YOURS
WITH THESE NEW BOOKS!

☐ **SINUSITIS, BRONCHITIS AND EMPHYSEMA**
(Clifford Quick) $1.95

☐ **YOUR BODY IS YOUR BEST DOCTOR**
(Melvin E. Page, D.D.S.) $1.25

☐ **GO AHEAD AND LIVE** (Mildred Loomis) 95¢

☐ **KNOW YOUR NUTRITION** (Linda Clark) $3.50

☐ **RECIPE FOR SURVIVAL** (Doris Grant) $3.95

☐ **YOUR KEYS TO RADIANT HEALTH**
(William E. Dankenbring) $1.95

☐ **THE HEALING NEEDLES** (Charles Ewart) $1.25

☐ **HEALING BENEFITS OF ACUPRESSURE**
(F.M. Houston, D.C.) $4.95

☐ **YOUR NATURAL HEALTH SAMPLER**
(Linda Clark and others) $1.25

☐ **YOUR WATER AND YOUR HEALTH**
(Allen E. Banik and Carlson Wade) $1.25

☐ **EAT THE WEEDS** (Ben Charles Harris) $1.25

☐ **DIET HEALTH CARD** (T.L. Cleave, M.D.) $1.00

Buy them at your local health or book store or use this coupon.

Keats Publishing, Inc. (P.O. Box 876), New Canaan, Conn. 06840   75
Please send me the books I have checked above. I am enclosing
$____ (add 35¢ to cover postage and handling). Send check or
money order—no cash or C.O.D.'s please.

Mr/Mrs/Miss____ _____

Address _____

City _____State _____Zip_____
(Allow three weeks for delivery)

The Best in Health Books by
LINDA CLARK,
BEATRICE TRUM HUNTER
and CARLSON WADE

By Linda Clark

☐ **Know Your Nutrition**   **$4.95**
☐ **Face Improvement Through Nutrition**   **$2.25**
☐ **Be Slim and Healthy**   **$1.50**
☐ **Go-Caution-Stop Carbohydrate Computer**   **$1.95**
☐ **The Best of Linda Clark**   **$4.50**
☐ **How to Improve Your Health**   **$4.95**

By Beatrice Trum Hunter

☐ **Whole Grain Baking Sampler**
    ☐ **Cloth $6.95**   ☐ **Paperback $2.95**
☐ **Additives Book**   **$2.25**
☐ **Fermented Foods and Beverages**   **$1.25**
☐ **Yogurt, Kefir & Other Milk Cultures**   **$1.75**
☐ **Wheat, Millet and Other Grains**   **$1.45**
☐ **High Power Foods**   **$1.45**

By Carlson Wade

☐ **Arthritis and Nutrition**   **$1.95**
☐ **Bee Pollen**   **$2.50**
☐ **Lecithin**   **$2.25**
☐ **Fats, Oils and Cholesterol**   **$1.50**
☐ **Vitamins and Other Supplements**   **$1.50**
☐ **Hypertension (High Blood Pressure)**   **$1.95**
   and Your Diet

Buy them at your local health or book store or use this coupon.

Keats Publishing, Inc. (P.O. Box 876), New Canaan, Conn. 06840   75-A
Please send me the books I have checked above. I am enclosing
$_____ (add $1.00 to cover postage and handling). Send check
or money order — no cash or C.O.D.'s please.

Mr/Mrs/Miss _____

Address_____

City_____ State_____ Zip_____
     (Allow three weeks for delivery)